The Leyland Atlantean

GAVIN BOOTH

NOSTALGIA ROAD

First published by Crécy Publishoing Ltd 2015

A CIP record for this book is available from the British Library

ISBN 9781908 347411

Printed in Bulgaria by Multiprint

Nostalgia Road is an imprint of Crécy Publishing Limited
1a Ringway Trading Estate
Shadowmoss Road
Manchester M22 5LH
www.crecy.co.uk

Front Cover: Portsmouth Corporation bought more than 150 Atlanteans over 18 years. This 1966 PDR1/1 has Metro-Cammell 76-seat bodywork to the style first introduced in 1958. *Ted Jones*

Back cover main image: This 1974 East Yorkshire AN68.1R with Park Royal 73-seat body Is seen at North Frodingham in 1979. *Tony Wilson*

Back cover Inset images clockwise from top:
The AN68A.1R 79-seater was an exhibit at the 1978 Commercial Show and features a dramatic front-end treatment with Nottingham's trademark narrow entrance and HELP bumper. *Tony Wilson*

One of the Quito Atlanteans is seen in service a long way from Leyland and Falkirk, and looking well used. *Julian Osborne*

Open-top Atlanteans were still running for Sevirama in Seville, Spain, in October 2012, including this 38-year-old former Nottingham AN68.1R with open-top East Lancs 76-seat body. *Gavin Booth*

Great Yarmouth bought the first Atlanteans to receive single-deck bodies – three PDR1/1s with 31ft-long Marshall 39-seat bodies. *Ted Jones/Tony Wilson*

Leicester City Transport took three of these 77-seat Metro-Cammellbodied PDR1/1s in 1962. *Geoffrey Morant*

This underframe view of Atlantean prototype 281 ATC illustrates its revolutionary features – including the independently sprung front wheels and drop-centre rear axle.

One of the Manila Atlanteans in service. Note 'destination' showing 'Metro Manila'. *BCVM*

CONTENTS

INTRODUCTION 4

1 BEFORE THE ATLANTEAN 5

2 THE ATLANTEAN APPEARS 12

3 INTO SERVICE 21

4 IMPROVEMENTS AND NEW
VARIATIONS 29

5 NEW CUSTOMERS 35

6 CHANGES ALL ROUND 45

7 LOOKING TO THE FUTURE 57

8 BORROWED TIME 60

9 EXPORT SUCCESS 68

10 THE ATLANTEAN ASSESSED 80

11 ATLANTEAN BODYBUILDERS 93

12 TESTING THE ATLANTEAN 101

13 THE ATLANTEAN IN ADVERTS 105

ATLANTEAN SPECIFICATIONS 108

INDEX 110

Colour photos of 281 ATC have proved elusive, but transport artist G S Cooper painted this in 1992 for *Classic Bus* magazine, showing the Atlantean prototype in service with Ribble in Liverpool. *G S Cooper*

Introduction

It is no exaggeration to say that the Leyland Atlantean revolutionised the design and layout of double-deck buses when it was first shown to the world in 1956, but even then it was so different that many of the more conservative bus operators must have had strong reservations about it, and there were naysayers who predicted that buses like this were just a passing phase and would never catch on.

They did catch on, of course, but there were many operators who resisted the Atlantean for more than a decade and continued to favour more conventional double-deckers with their engines planted firmly at the front. Yet even these owed a lot to Leyland, which in 1927 had introduced its low-built Titan, a name that would grace a succession of double-deck models right through to the late 1960s, and would be revived in the 1970s. In 1956, when the Atlantean was launched, Leyland's Titan was competing with double-deck chassis from AEC, Daimler, Dennis and Guy, while Bristol double-deck chassis were restricted to state-owned companies, and Midland Red built its own buses.

Leyland's customers in the UK were the municipal and independent sectors, as well as the BET Group and the state-owned London Transport and Scottish Bus Group. But Leyland had built up a substantial export business and was also selling Titans into some of these markets – though typically it was Leyland's single-deck models that sold best overseas.

For a teenage schoolboy in 1956, the first glimpse in *Buses Illustrated* magazine of photographs of the Atlantean was nothing short of a revelation. This sleek-looking bus was surely the future, but of course that first Atlantean, registered 281 ATC by Leyland as a demonstrator, turned out not to be what customers really wanted. Leyland had to swiftly rethink the concept and come up with a revised model in 1958.

Just to see and ride on an Atlantean became an important goal for me, and fortunately one of the first production models was ordered by Glasgow Corporation and could be found little more than an hour's journey from my Edinburgh home. Newcastle Corporation was another early customer, so day trips to north-east England became part of the routine, particularly when the Northern General companies also started to place Atlanteans in service.

We now know that some of these early Atlanteans had teething problems that gave the model a reputation that allowed the conservatives to say, 'I told you so.' But Leyland addressed these problems, something that became even more urgent when Daimler introduced its Fleetline in 1960, offering some features that the Atlantean did not have – notably the engineers' favourite Gardner engine and a lowheight layout that permitted normal seating on both decks, important for operators where bridges and depots restricted the overall height of a double-decker.

None of this, though, should take away from the importance of the Atlantean – very much the father of the modern double-decker. And if Leyland got a few things wrong in its pioneering efforts, it put them all right with the hugely successful AN68-series Atlantean, which sold in impressive quantities to satisfied customers for more than a decade.

My thanks go to Michael Eyre and Richard Morant, who assisted with the photographic content, both in terms of making photos from the Roy Marshall and Geoffrey Morant collections available and also for working their magic on slides that were up to half a century old.

Various publications from the PSV Circle have proved invaluable in confirming details of Atlantean production.

Gavin Booth
Edinburgh

Before the Atlantean

There was nothing new about rear-engined buses; they existed long before the Atlantean. Manufacturers in the United States were building rear-engined buses in the 1930s – including double-deckers – and, in Britain, Leyland itself was looking at alternatives to the near-universal front-engined layout for single-deck and double-deck buses and coaches.

The Atlantean was as much of a sensation as Leyland's Titan TD1 had been in 1927, pioneering the basic layout for generations of double-deckers. This preserved Glasgow Corporation 1928 TD1 with lowbridge Leyland bodywork was one of the first of hundreds of Titans bought by Glasgow over the next 34 years, after which Glasgow moved decisively to Leyland's new Atlantean. *Gavin Booth*

Leyland gained first-hand experience of rear-engined buses in the late 1930s when it developed its REC chassis for London Transport. This was a version of the front-engined Cub it already supplied to LT for lighter, driver-only routes, but with a Leyland 4. 4-litre diesel engine mounted vertically at the rear, in line with the chassis. LT built the 20-seat bodies for the 46 REC types delivered in 1937-39 as LT's CR class. In spite of the engine position, the CR retained a halfcab arrangement at the front; this layout would be echoed nearly 20 years later in LFDD prototype XTC 684. This is the preserved CR14, seen at Chiswick in 1983. *Tony Wilson*

The Titan PD2 was a popular and reliable chassis, and Leyland emphasised the longevity of the O.600 engine in adverts like this 1957 example, highlighting Stockton Corporation PD2s that were well on the way to achieving 400,000 miles in service. *All uncredited photographs come from official sources or are from the author's collection*

In 1936, Leyland built a rear-engined prototype with a petrol engine mounted transversely behind the rear axle. Midland Red had built a rear-engined bus in 1935 – which may have prompted Leyland's actions – and while Leyland's bus was never tried in service, it gave the company useful experience of this layout.

Leyland was also looking at the underfloor-engined layout for single-deckers, and in 1937 worked with London Transport (LT) to develop a prototype bus to this layout, which was followed in 1939 by 87 production examples. LT had been experimenting with resiting the engine on its new bus models and had developed the side-engined Q with AEC, its main collaborator and chassis supplier, and Leyland's greatest rival.

But Leyland was chosen to develop a new rear-engined type for driver-only operation on suburban and rural routes. In 1934-36, LT had bought over a hundred of Leyland's normal control Cub chassis to replace the variety of small buses inherited when the London Passenger Transport Board was formed in 1933. In 1937, LT came back to Leyland, which developed a rear-engined version of the Cub, with a diesel engine mounted at the rear, inline with the chassis. Following trials with the 1937 prototype, a further 45 rear-engined Cubs were delivered between September 1939 and February 1940, by which time World War 2 had started and the opportunity for further developments along these lines was put on hold.

After the war, Britain's bus manufacturers were being urged to export much of their production to help the postwar economy, while at the same time UK bus operators were desperate for new buses to replace the many older prewar vehicles that would otherwise have long since been withdrawn but had been kept on the road in order to keep the country moving in wartime. Leyland's peacetime double-deck offering was initially the Titan PD1, a conventional front-engined chassis with a new 7.4-litre engine. The PD1 family sold well to hungry bus operators, but Leyland's next double-deck range would soon appear – the PD2 series – with another new engine, the 9.8-litre O.600.

The PD2 initially offered a gearbox with synchromesh on most gears, but there was an increasing interest in preselective transmission in several of the larger municipal fleets, and automatic gearboxes were on the horizon. LT's large postwar fleet of RT-family double-deckers, including over 2,000 Leylands based on the Titan PD2, all had preselectors, as had Birmingham's postwar standard Daimlers and Guys. Indeed, at this time Daimler offered only preselective transmission. But while Leyland was prepared to adapt its specification to include preselector boxes, it was more interested in moving to two-pedal control, and with Self-Changing Gears Ltd of Coventry it developed what it called the Pneumocyclic gearbox, a four-speed (later five-speed) epicyclic box that was controlled by a miniature lever but required no clutch pedal. It was offered as a semi-automatic box on the Titan range from 1954, and in fully automatic form from 1956.

So now two of the main ingredients for the Atlantean – the O.600 engine and the Pneumocyclic gearbox – were in place, but for a time Leyland did not seem to acknowledge this.

Leyland's single-deck range had changed completely in the early 1950s when the front-engined Tiger models were joined by – and quickly replaced by – underfloor-engined types: the Olympic, Royal Tiger and Tiger Cub. These gave operators the chance to buy buses with up to 45 seats in the 30ft overall length that was legal in the UK at the time. With a horizontal engine tucked under the floor between the axles, there was no engine intrusion into the passenger saloon. The downside was that floor levels were high and passengers had to negotiate several steps into the buses.

The overall height of double-deckers has always been important to bus builders. With a 'normal-height' double-decker around 14ft 6in (4.42m) high and operators with low bridge or depot problems looking for double-deckers no higher than 13ft 6in (4.12m), the holy grail was a 13ft 6in-high bus with normal seating on both decks. The existing solution, really since Leyland's lowbridge Titan in 1927, was a slightly awkward upper deck with a sunken side gangway and four-across seating at a higher level. Nobody pretended that this was the perfect solution, but in 1927 it allowed operators to use double-deckers more widely. However, by the 1950s, passengers were growing increasingly unhappy with the cramped and awkward upper saloon seats.

Bristol and Eastern Coach Works (ECW) had come up with an ingenious solution in 1949 – the Lodekka – which offered normal seating on both decks by using a drop-centre rear axle. Although the Lodekka was available only to state-owned fleets, other manufacturers, including Leyland itself, would develop models in a similar mould.

As underfloor-engined double-deckers were not going to provide the answer – although Midland Red and, later, Volvo and Leyland would offer double-deckers with underfloor engines, with mixed success – in 1952, the Leyland engineers turned back to the concept of rear-mounted engines.

The double-decker of the time was invariably front-engined with the driver in a halfcab alongside the engine, and

From the front there was little indication that Leyland LFDD STF 90 would be the starting-point for generations of double-deck buses. The absence of a front radiator gave the Saunders-Roe body a trolleybus-like appearance, and as the engine was mounted on the rear wall of the open platform it was not immediately apparent how revolutionary this bus was. The door that can be seen in the centre of the bulkhead behind the driver gave access to the cab. *Michael Dryhurst*

Even from the rear, only the cooling grille at the rear provided any clue that STF 90 was a revolutionary bus. It was photographed when on demonstration to Southdown in July 1954, painted in a livery close to the Southdown green and cream. *Michael Dryhurst*

Lowland Motorways, which operated a largely second-hand fleet in suburban Glasgow, bought both of the Leyland LFDD prototypes in 1957, but they were sold on when the business was acquired by Scottish Omnibuses in 1958. STF 90 is seen in Lowland service in 1957. *Geoffrey Morant*

when bodied it was up to 27ft (8.23m) long, 8ft (2.44m) wide and normally had a passenger entrance behind the rear axle, sometimes with doors but mostly without. The seating capacity of many of these conventional double-deckers had crept up from 56 to 60, and there were operators working hard to squeeze more seats in; the new LT Routemaster in 1954 was a 64-seater, for example, and some bus companies managed to get the seating capacity up to 66. Maximising seating capacity was an important goal, and late in 1952, Leyland built an

Left: The second LFDD, Metro-Cammell-bodied XTC 684, had not previously been used in public service and is seen at Lowland's yard in Shettleston, Glasgow, in 1957, flanked by two 1944 ex-Western SMT utility Daimler CWA6s with Brush bodies. Despite being just a few years old, neither LFDD passed to Scottish Omnibuses in 1958, although the two Daimlers did. The different front end of XTC will be noted; the fuel tank and batteries were housed in the area to the driver's left. *Geoffrey Morant*

Below: A rare photo of the two LFDDs, posed together at the terminus of Lowland's Garthamlock route in east Glasgow. The very different approaches to bodying these buses – Saunders-Roe on STF 90 and Metro-Cammell on XTC 684 – will be noted. *Ian Maclean*

The second LFDD prototype, XTC 684, passed to Buckmaster of Leighton Buzzard. It is now preserved. *Geoffrey Morant*

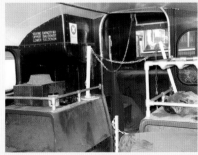

LFDD MkII XTC 684 is now in the North West Museum of Road Transport in St Helens. The detail photos show the forward view of the lower deck showing the driver's access from the saloon, the view towards the lower deck rear with the stairs and black rounded top of the engine compartment, and the engine compartment itself. *Gavin Booth*

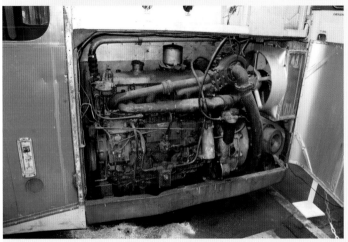

experimental model that has come to be known as the Lowloader, although this name does not appear to have been used by Leyland. A contemporary internal report describes it as the 'Low Floor Double Deck Bus Chassis', shortened to LFDD, which is used in this book in the interests of accuracy.

A platform was built with a flat lower-deck floor and the engine mounted right at the rear, actually on what would be the open platform. The engine was not the trusty O.600, which would have taken up far too much room in this layout and affected axle weights, but a gently turbocharged version of Leyland's recently introduced 5.7-litre O.350 unit. The gearbox chosen for the LFDD was an equally interesting choice, a Wilson preselector. In 1952, Leyland had fitted a prewar Birmingham City Transport Leyland Titan with an O.350 engine and Wilson box, and this had run in Birmingham and Edinburgh in 1952-54, possibly in connection with the development of the rear-engined double-decker. Certainly Leyland's Research Department was known to be interested in smaller turbocharged engines at the time.

Early in 1953, Leyland had set up a new development and research division under Dr-Ing A Müller to look at long-term design plans. The design committee laid down general specifications for a rear-engined double-decker: it would be required to have a low-platform front entrance under control of the driver, leaving the conductor free to concentrate on fare collection in view of the potentially large passenger-carrying capacity, and the engine would be at the rear, but the frame needed to be low and step-free to satisfy lowheight needs. The LFDD did not meet all of these requirements, but it was a useful test-bed that allowed Leyland to gain first-hand experience of a rear-engined double-decker.

The prototype Atlantean LFDD MkIII, 281 ATC with Metro-Cammell lowheight body, created a sensation when it was unveiled in 1956. Although the bodywork has some echoes of the controversial Orion design, its lines are well proportioned and clean. Note the thicker pillars, no doubt because of concerns about structural rigidity on such an innovative design, and the curved glass on the driver's windscreen.

Ribble was a prime target customer for the Atlantean, and prototype 281 ATC is seen at Crosby bus station during trials on Ribble's L3 route between Crosby and Liverpool. *Ken Swallow*

The LFDD prototype was bodied by Saunders-Roe with a full-width cab, rather like a trolleybus, and a rear open platform with the engine at the extreme rear. The 61-seat alloy body helped achieve an excellent total unladen weight of 6.85 tons (6959kg), with a creditable overall height of 13ft 3in (4.04m). It was registered STF 90 as a Leyland demonstrator and was placed in service in 1954.

E J Smith, writing in the magazine *Buses Illustrated* for January-March 1955, referred to the appearance of STF 90 in the demonstration park at the 1954 Commercial Motor Show and to Leyland's reluctance to say anything about the new vehicle. However, he gleaned details from various sources and managed a trip in the bus. He was 'most impressed by the short ride. Suspension was really excellent, although only about a dozen people were aboard. The engine is not unduly loud with no noticeable whine from the blower (it is in fact much quieter than the standard Comet) and there was very little vibration. Acceleration was above average, and, steering exceptionally light – something which will be more than welcomed by a good many bus drivers.'

John Smith felt that 'Leyland definitely have something out of the ordinary in the LFDD, and it will be interesting to see how the various unorthodox features work in practice, and whether this vehicle will offer a solution to the low bridge problem. As with other designs in the same mould, time will tell.'

The monthly magazine *Bus & Coach* described the LFDD as 'a courageous break with accepted practice ... but although the bus has been given service trials by several passenger transport undertakings it cannot yet be said to have passed from the experimental stage to one from which its regular production can be expected in the immediate future. It is, however, an outstanding example of the advanced thinking now being accorded double-deck development.'

Inside Earls Court at the 1954 show was RM1, the prototype LT Routemaster, which, in spite of its more conventional external appearance, positively bristled with new features. It was integrally constructed, lacking a separate chassis as such, but was instead built around two steel sub-frames – the front one carrying the engine and front suspension assembly, and the rear sub-frame the rear axle and suspension. But it still had the engine at the front and an open platform at the rear.

LFDD prototype STF 90 was inspected by several operators in 1954, mainly BET Group fleets like Devon General, Potteries, Ribble and Southdown, and was subsequently used in service by several of Leyland's target customers.

A second LFDD underframe was built in 1954, similar to STF 90 but with a Pneumocyclic gearbox. It was bodied by Metro-Cammell with a halfcab front, rather like the prewar rear-engined Cubs for LT, although in place of an engine the area to the driver's left housed the batteries and the diesel tank. Registered XTC 684, this bus was initially used by Leyland for testing and development and did not enter public service until 1957 when it was sold, along with STF 90, to the Glasgow independent operator Lowland Motorways. STF 90 passed to Buckmaster of Leighton Buzzard after Lowland was acquired by Scottish Omnibuses Ltd in 1958, and was scrapped in 1963 after working with Strowger of Manchester. XTC 684 also passed from Lowland to Buckmaster, and survives in the North West Museum of Road Transport in St Helens. Another LFSD underframe was produced in 1956, a low-floor single-deck bus, but this was never bodied and was scrapped in 1956. These prototypes were what today would be called 'concept vehicles', built to test the water and gauge the reaction of potential customers.

The next concept vehicle moved the story on dramatically. This was 281 ATC, arguably the father of the modern double-deck bus, unveiled in the autumn of 1956 as the Atlantean – the result of Leyland's four-year development programme.

The lower deck of 281 ATC, looking to the rear, with its gently sloping flat floor and the bulkheads behind the rear wheels – no doubt a structural feature as Metro-Cammell got to grips with the different stresses of a heavy rear-mounted engine.

The upper deck view of 281 ATC is more conventional, with a rearward-ascending staircase and a single seat opposite the stairs.

The Atlantean appears

Bus operators had been lobbying for longer double-deckers in their efforts to increase seating capacity. Single-deckers were now routinely 30ft (9.14m) long, but two-axle double-deckers were restricted to 27ft (8.23m), and only three-axle double-deckers could be built to the 30ft length. Walsall Corporation had received special dispensation to operate two-axle 30ft-long Sunbeam double-deck trolleybuses in 1954, and these helped to make the case for a universal relaxation of the legislation.

Some Leyland fans resisted the Atlantean for as long as they could and continued to buy Titans. Southdown built up a fleet of PD3s with Northern Counties forward-entrance bodies, the legendary 'Queen Marys', and these featured a full-front design giving them a more contemporary look. This 1965 Southdown PD3 was sold to OK Motor Services of Bishop Auckland for further service and is seen at its home depot alongside an OK Atlantean/Northern Counties. *Gavin Booth*

Although 30ft two-axle double-deckers became legal only from 1 July 1956, manufacturers had known this was coming and had planned their new models accordingly. For Leyland's staple Titan range it was a fairly simple step to lengthen the popular PD2 to become the PD3. But for the team working on the rear-engined double-deck project, the new legislation was a godsend. Now they could make better use of the space available and design a model with an entrance ahead of the front wheels, beside the driver. This got away from the awkward rear platform layout of the LFDD prototypes and set the fashion for virtually every new double-deck model since.

The results of Leyland's revised thinking were unveiled at the 1956 Commercial Motor Show at Earls Court, London. The LFDD had morphed into the Atlantean, a sleek lowheight bus that at a stroke made other double-deckers look positively out of date.

Leyland had worked with Metro-Cammell to produce a semi-integral vehicle just 13ft 3in (4.04m) high, the low overall height being achieved by independent front suspension and a drop-centre rear axle. The set-back front wheels allowed an entrance door right at the front, and the engine was contained within the rear end structure. There were 78 seats, and it weighed just 7.75 tons (7874kg). Gone was the turbocharged O.350 engine, and the popular O.600 was at the back, with a semi-automatic Pneumocyclic gearbox.

The name Atlantean – pertaining to Atlas or Atlantis – was in line with the mythologically derived Titan and was represented on Atlantean badging with Atlas, the primordial Titan who held up the earth, kneeling with a globe on his shoulders.

Bus operators who inspected the bus at Earls Court were generally positive. Ben England, then General Manager of Nottingham City Transport, wrote in the trade monthly *Bus & Coach* that he thought the Atlantean was 'probably more suitable for use on limited-stop services than on ordinary city services' and felt that 'some people would criticise the rather restricted circulating space near the front entrance, on to which the staircase gives'. The way round this, he suggested, was to sacrifice the three first nearside seats in the lower saloon, reducing the capacity to 75. E J Smith, writing in *Buses Illustrated*, also criticised the bottleneck at the foot of the stairs, which would prove to be a constant problem in production Atlanteans.

G W Hayter, former General Manager and Chief Engineer of the Northern General group of companies, was an advocate of front entrances for double-deckers, to allow drivers to supervise boarding and alighting passengers, leaving the conductor to concentrate on fare collection. At the time he wrote, 'This concentration is most desirable where seats are provided for more than 50 or 60 passengers. With 70-plus seats such an arrangement is absolutely essential.'

Mr Hayter also raised the question of Leyland's apparent preoccupation with producing an all-purpose lowheight bus. 'Why, oh why,' he wrote, 'has Leyland tried to do too much? In the laudable

Until the Atlantean came on stream, bus operators looking to maximise seating capacity bought models like Leyland's Titan PD3, built to the recently legalised 30ft length. This 1958 advert features a 1957 Potteries PD3/4 with Metro-Cammell forward-entrance 68-seat bodywork. Many operators turned to forward entrances for their 30ft double-deckers, and, as here, some continued to specify the exposed-radiator variants rather than chassis with full-width fronts.

aim of trying to gain maximum capacity as well as to lower the height of the vehicle the lower-deck seating arrangements are unattractive. Surely it would have been enough to have produced a front-entrance double-decker of normal height and, having accustomed the public to the new type of entrance, to have gone forward with the production of a type able to go through low bridges, but not with the seating arrangements as seen at the Exhibition. If anything can kill an innovation with enormous possibilities, which the public and operators are asked to accept, the

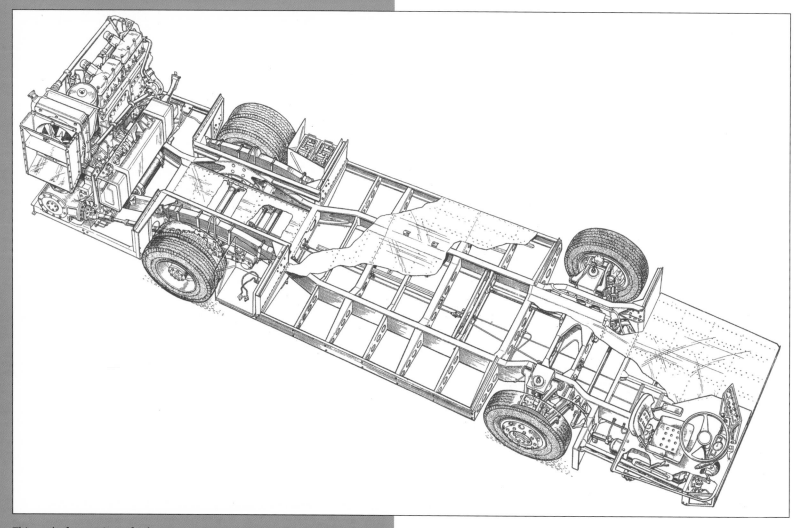

This underframe view of Atlantean prototype 281 ATC illustrates its revolutionary features – including the transversely mounted O. 600 engine and semi-automatic gearbox, the independently sprung front wheels and the drop-centre rear axle that permitted the overall height to be just 13ft 3in.

A contemporary illustration shows the low floor line of Atlantean prototype 281 ATC.

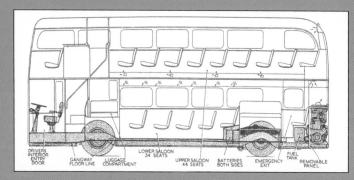

lower-deck seating arrangements will do it in spite of the fact that the vehicle has the good name of Leyland behind it.'

The innovative Bristol/ECW Lodekka, first seen in 1949, and available only to state firms, showed that a lowheight bus could have normal seating on both decks, but there was clearly a limited demand for lowheight double-deckers and while Leyland would tackle it in a fairly unsatisfactory way on production Atlanteans, Daimler soon showed how to do it with its rear-engined Fleetline double-decker launched in 1960. More than anything, longer single-deckers, sometimes with as many seats as a lowbridge double-decker, would offer operators a more practical alternative.

The prototype Atlantean was registered 281 ATC and acted as a Leyland demonstrator, operating in service with municipal and BET Group fleets around the country. Intensive service with real passengers and a variety of drivers quickly identify weaknesses in any bus, and bus companies fed their responses back to Leyland. In his book *The Leyland Bus*, Doug Jack listed some of the shortcomings:

'Although the concept was brilliant, there were too many drawbacks to enable the bus to be placed on the market. The noise level at the rear of the lower saloon was excessive, largely because the engine was inside the bus. The floor was just too low, and the independent front suspension was practically at the limit of its capacity. Production models would have been prohibitively dear in comparison to the competition, and there was always the apathy of the British operator to integral construction.'

There was a second 'MkIII' Atlantean, an unregistered bus that bore the chassis number 562095 following that of 281 ATC, but while it was seen around the Leyland plant, it was scrapped, as, sadly, was 281 ATC, in the mid-1960s. The MkIII designation reflected that this was the third stage in the experiments, but these early prototypes could more sensibly be described as PDR1s.

Atlantean 281 ATC was used to develop the breed in the light of reactions from bus operators who had shown that they liked the broad concept but still expressed misgivings, and so Leyland engineers went back to the drawing board. Leyland was still keen to steer its customers towards complete buses and while that time would come, for the moment they bit the bullet and redesigned the Atlantean as a separate chassis, following rigorous testing that had caused cracks in the underframe of 281 ATC and its unregistered sister at the MIRA proving ground.

In the development process 281 ATC lost its drop-centre rear axle in favour of a more conventional one, and this required the rear of the upper deck to be rebuilt to allow headroom in the lower deck to meet the legal minimum. Leyland's solution was a raised platform at the rear of the upper deck with gangways at each side and three-across bench seating, reducing the upper-deck seats from 44 to 37. This, perhaps sensibly, did not turn out to be the way Leyland achieved low overall height in production Atlanteans.

Externally, the rear of 281 ATC was rebuilt to enclose the engine, transmission and radiator in an externally mounted cowling, the first appearance of the lift-up canopy that created the familiar notch-back look of early Atlanteans and Daimler Fleetlines.

As originally conceived, the Atlantean engine was within the bodywork rather than in a 'power pack' at the rear, and this view shows how the engine and gearbox were shoehorned into the space behind the rear axle. Although access was straightforward, the engine layout proved to be noisy for passengers. The roof-mounted exhaust outlet was a feature that would not be carried over on to production Atlanteans.

A detail from a Leyland official photograph shows 281 ATC's unregistered LFDD MkIII sister of 1956, sitting in the yard at Leyland's South Works. This was the bus used for testing at the MIRA track that led to the rethinking of the whole Atlantean project. *BVMVA*

In its first flush of enthusiasm for the Atlantean, Leyland placed this advert in the trade press in November 1956, although the critical feedback from operators that caused Leyland to revisit the whole Atlantean concept meant that there would be no more adverts for the model for another couple of years.

The first public indication that the Atlantean was about to be reborn came in this MCW advert that appeared in the trade press in June 1958. It shows a probably fictitious Atlantean that combines the lower front panel of 281 ATC with the style of bodywork that would become very familiar, complete with the 'bustle' at the back for the engine compartment. Although by this time 281 ATC had been rebuilt with the 'bustle', the evenly spaced side windows were more akin to production Atlanteans than to the two 1956 prototypes with their thick structural pillars. The copy in the advert seems to imply that the Atlantean is an MCW product that just happens to have Leyland running units – hardly the case.

The mechanical components were largely the same, but the production Atlantean chassis lost the independent front suspension and drop-centre rear axle in favour of conventional axles, and Leyland had to abandon its dream of a universal double-decker to a low overall height and accept that most customers would be happy with a normal-height bus. Operators requiring buses built to a lower height could be accommodated in some other way.

So Leyland had four pre-production Atlantean PDR1/1s to exhibit at the 1958 Commercial Show: two were 14ft 6in (4.42m) normal-height buses and two were 13ft 4in (4.06m) high. The semi-lowbridge layout of 281 ATC was replaced with an arrangement whereby the rearmost four rows of seats in the upper deck were on a platform with a gangway to the nearside, with seating typically for 73 (39 up, 34 down, compared with the maximum 44/34 arrangement of normal-height Atlanteans). It was not the most satisfactory arrangement but it allowed several early customers to buy Atlanteans. The situation would change when competition appeared on the scene in the shape of the Daimler Fleetline.

Alexander and Metropolitan-Cammell-Weymann (MCW) were entrusted with the bodies on the four 1958 Show Atlanteans and bodied 78-seat normal-height buses for Glasgow and Wallasey corporations respectively; MCW built 73-seat semi-lowbridge bodies for two BET companies, Maidstone & District and J James of Ammanford. The bodies on the James bus, and on the first batch for James, were apparently built by Metro-Cammell at Elmdon, Birmingham, although all further semi-lowbridge Atlantean bodies would be built by Weymann at Addlestone in Surrey.

Externally, the bodies on the new Atlantean chassis were broadly the same as on 1956 prototype 281 ATC but perhaps lacked the sleekness of the semi-integral bus. The most noticeable difference was the engine compartment in its 'bustle' at the back, which was designed for easy access during maintenance and relatively easy replacement of major units.

The MCW bodies were fairly uninspired, with echoes of the much-criticised Metro-Cammell Orion bodywork, having shallow upper-deck windows and (on the normal-height buses) deeper lower-deck ones. The front ends were flat, and for many it was the sheer novelty that attracted them to the Atlantean rather than its good looks. The proportions of the Alexander-bodied Glasgow bus were broadly the same as the Metro-Cammell version but with a slightly softer outline.

The more adventurous operators placed orders for the new Atlantean, while others, including some that would become major customers, held back to see how the model worked in urban service. But with orders for over 200 chassis, the Atlantean was well and truly on its way.

Two of the four Atlantean PDR1/1s that appeared at the 1958 Commercial Motor Show came together again in 1986 for an open day at the Greenock depot of Clydeside Scottish. These are the two normal-height buses – Wallasey Corporation 1 with Metro-Cammell body and Glasgow Corporation LA1 with Alexander body. *Gavin Booth*

Wallasey Corporation, a committed Leyland customer, went on to buy a total of 30 Atlantean PDR1/1s with 77-seat Metro-Cammell bodies in 1958-61. These are 1960 examples, seen in 1968. *Ted Jones*

A semi-lowheight Maidstone & District PDR1/1 with MCW bodywork was at the 1958 show, and M&D bought over 150 Atlanteans in 1958-63 before switching its allegiance to the new Daimler Fleetline. This is one of the 1959 semi-lowheight 73-seaters, seen in 1969. *Ted Jones*

The other semi-lowheight MCW-bodied PDR1/1 Atlantean at the 1958 show was this bus for the BET company, J James of Ammanford.

The bulk deliveries of Alexander-bodied Atlanteans for Glasgow Corporation had the attractive style of body carried by this 1968 PDR1 78-seater seen in 1973 being passed by a 1959 Leyland Titan PD2/24 with 61-seat Alexander body, representing the old order. *Gavin Booth*

The chassis of the production PDR1/1 Atlantean showed that Leyland had abandoned some of the more advanced features like the independent front suspension and the drop-centre rear axle and produced a model that would suit the majority of its customers who wanted a normal-height bus. The 'power pack' housing the engine and gearbox was probably the most obvious change from the 1956 prototype.

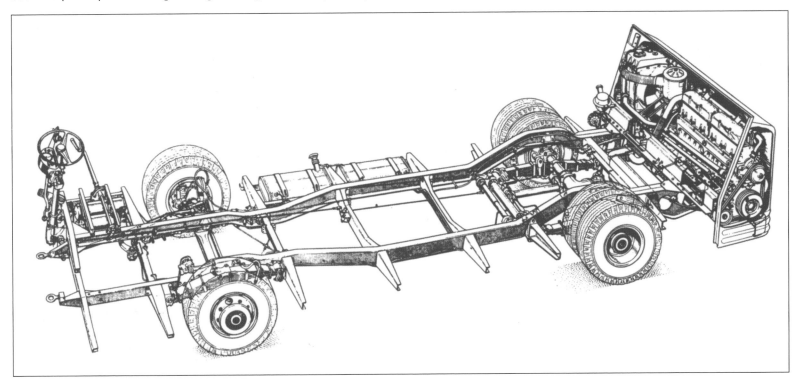

Leyland's solution to the demand for a lowheight Atlantean was this slightly awkward layout, conceived in conjunction with MCW and normally built by Weymann at Addlestone. Lacking a drop-centre rear axle, the headroom was reduced at the rear of the lower deck, so the seats on the deck above had to be mounted on a raised platform, with four rows of four-across seating at the rear to achieve an overall height of 13ft 4in.

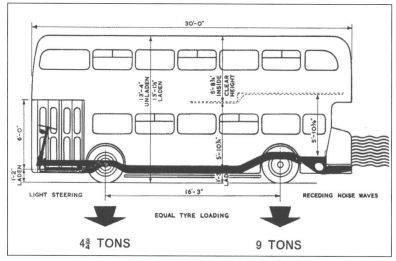

Leyland released this image to show the internal dimensions of a semi-lowheight Atlantean/Weymann and the loading on the two axles for a fully laden bus.

Into service

Leyland knew that only first-hand experience of the Atlantean would help to convince some of the more sceptical operators, so among the first production Atlanteans to appear, in 1959, were demonstrators. There were three Metro-Cammell-bodied normal-height buses: 398 JTB, 46 LTB, and an unregistered bus that was used for trials by Leyland and Self-Changing Gears Ltd, its subsidiary since 1956. The British demonstrator was 398 JTB, with 46 LTB working in Ireland, and there was also a Weymann-bodied lowheight demonstrator, 661 KTJ. Another demonstrator was built in 1960, 460 MTE, with 71-seat Metro-Cammell body. It was constructed with Birmingham City Transport in mind, and BCT bought it in 1961.

Atlantean deliveries started in the spring of 1959 and gained momentum as the year went on. The privately owned BET Group, with operating companies throughout England and Wales, was an early customer, Atlanteans going to Devon General, East Midland, James, Maidstone & District, Mexborough & Swinton, Northern

The BET Devon General fleet was an early Atlantean customer. This is numerically the company's first example, a 1959 PDR1/1 with Metro-Cammell 76-seat body, seen in 1972 accompanied by an AEC Reliance and an AEC Regent V. Devon General was a committed AEC customer, and the Willowbrook-bodied Regent is six years younger than the Atlantean. *Royston Morgan*

BET's East Midland fleet required lowheight buses, and 32 of these PDR1/1 Atlanteans with Weymann 73-seat semi-lowheight bodies were bought in 1959/60. This 1959 example is at Nottingham in 1970. *Roy Marshall*

Northern General, another BET Group company, was an early Atlantean customer, taking examples for several of its subsidiaries from 1959. This is a 1962 Sunderland District PDR1/1 with uncharacteristically unattractive bodywork by Roe. *Roy Marshall*

General group companies, Potteries, Ribble, Trent, Western Welsh and Yorkshire Traction. From the start there was a good mix of Metro-Cammell normal-height and Weymann lowheight examples, with Maidstone & District and Trent taking both, while Devon General, Northern General and Ribble took only full-height buses; the rest took only lowheight buses at the time. Other early Metro-Cammell full-height customers were the municipal fleets at Great Yarmouth, Hull, Liverpool, Newcastle, Plymouth, Sheffield and Wallasey, while Chesterfield and Walsall took lowheights.

The first delivery to an independent operator was in 1959, to Silver Star Motor Services of Porton Down, which took a Weymann lowheight example, and early normal-height MCW Atlanteans went to J Laurie of Hamilton and Scout Motor Services of Preston.

Potteries was an enthusiastic customer for the semi-lowheight Atlantean – at least until the Daimler Fleetline came along. This is a 1959-delivered PDR1/1 with 73-seat Weymann body, still going strong in 1977. *Tony Wilson*

Two 1962 Ribble PDR1/1s with 72-seat semi-lowheight Weymann bodywork pass in Carlisle in 1979, showing the original style of engine compartment used on earlier Atlanteans. *Sholto Thomas*

Other bodybuilders started to body Atlanteans. Alexander built early deliveries for Northern General's Gateshead & District and Sunderland District subsidiaries as well as for Belfast, Newcastle and Sheffield corporations. The first Roe-bodied Atlanteans appeared in 1960 for BET's Devon General, Northern General and Trent fleets. These were all normal-height buses.

Ribble had a network of express services between north-west England and London, and one of its earliest Atlantean deliveries was particularly interesting. It was a double-deck coach designed to operate on the first British motorways being built at the time, which would allow faster journey times. So while Midland Red was developing high-speed single-deck coaches for the West Midlands to London run, Ribble had revisited the double-deck concept (between 1948 and 1951, it had bought 50 double-deck coaches based on Leyland Titan chassis and dubbed them 'White Ladies').

Ribble's new double-deck coach, the 'Gay Hostess', was built by Weymann and based on a standard normal-height Metro-Cammell Atlantean body with external embellishments that took away from the bus-like shell; there were 50 coach seats, a toilet, a servery and extra luggage space. It had air suspension in place of the normal leaf springs, and quickly received the newer 11.1-litre Leyland O.680 engine; it had a top speed of 64mph. It was joined by 14 further Ribble examples, and 22 others for Ribble's subsidiary Standerwick.

Looking at the fleets that rushed to buy these early Atlanteans, a few stayed faithful to the model right to the end of its life, some moved away to other types fairly quickly, and others seemed undecided about what to buy. Of the four companies whose buses appeared at the 1958 Show, Glasgow and Wallasey stayed with the Atlantean; James bought Atlanteans until it was merged into South Wales Transport; and Maidstone & District, after buying more than 150 Atlanteans in 1958-63, turned to Daimler's Fleetline. For many, the genuine lowheight body layout that was possible on the Fleetline chassis was a strong attraction, and some of the operators that bought semi-lowbridge Atlanteans in the early days would also desert Leyland for the Fleetline.

Daimler's rear-engined Fleetline double-deck chassis appeared at the end of 1960, but it was 1962 before production examples started to enter service so Leyland had a head start with the Atlantean. By the end of 1961, over 800 Atlanteans had entered service in the UK. Putting that into perspective, they represented just 15% of new double-deck deliveries. The best-sellers in these years were the Leyland Titan and AEC Routemaster.

The double-deck market was traditionally dominated by the two biggest manufacturers, AEC and Leyland, with AEC's sales buoyed by LT orders. Between them they represented around two-thirds of UK double-deck sales, with Bristol following at around 20% and BMMO, Daimler, Dennis and Guy accounting for most of the remainder.

Walsall Corporation, which had a reputation for trying new things, bought only one Atlantean – this 1959 PDR1/1 with Weymann 74-seat semi-lowheight bodywork, seen in 1970. Walsall went on to buy Daimler Fleetlines, but opted for a short-wheelbase version to its own specification. *Geoffrey Morant*

same year Daimler passed into Jaguar control; Guy followed the next year. With investment to ramp up production, sales of Daimler's Fleetline were almost level with Leyland's Atlantean by 1963, and the Fleetline actually outsold the Atlantean in 1964 and 1967.

Flushed with the early success of the Atlantean, Leyland designed a rear-engined single-deck chassis, the Lion, an export model that combined elements of the Atlantean and the hugely successful mid-engined Worldmaster. Like the Atlantean, the O.600 or O.680 engine was mounted in what Leyland described as a 'power pack' but unlike the Atlantean it did not sell well, despite deliveries to the United States, Australia, New Zealand, Spain, Turkey – and Iran, which turned out to be its largest market. Some of the Australian Lions

Leyland's highest percentage share in the 1950s and 1960s was 51% of the UK double-deck market in 1958, with over 900 sales of its front-engined Titan. Although the Atlantean came on stream in 1959, the Titan would continue to outsell it until 1962 and Titan deliveries fell away for the rest of the decade. AEC's best year in the 1960s was 1960 when it had 33% of the market, but its double-deck sales declined following the AEC-Leyland 'merger' in 1962. Although AEC and LT developed a prototype rear-engined Routemaster in the mid-1960s and there were plans to sell these to fleets outside London, the bus remained the solitary example of its type as Leyland's thoughts turned to developing a truly universal double-decker that would be acceptable in London, the rest of the UK – and ideally throughout the world. However, it would be another decade before this was unveiled.

Daimler, on the other hand, had never been a high-volume bus builder and its long-running CV range had dwindled to double-figure annual sales by the time the Fleetline was introduced in 1960, the

were three-axle chassis, but the Lion went out of production in 1967. By that time Leyland had introduced two new rear-engined single-deckers: the Panther, with a rear-mounted horizontal O.600 engine; and the Panther Cub, with an O.400 engine. These first appeared in 1964, but while the Panther enjoyed reasonable success it was not until Leyland and National Bus Company got together to develop the integral Leyland National, launched in 1970, that significant rear-engined single-deck sales were made.

The rear-engined double-decker did not sound an immediate death-knell for its front-engined predecessor; in fact, front-engined models dominated the UK double-deck market until 1966 and it was only in 1968 that the Atlantean and Fleetline had the market virtually to themselves. And it was not just because they were the chassis bus operators were desperate to buy. There were still operators who liked the simplicity and reliability of models like the AEC Regent, Daimler CV, Guy Arab and Leyland Titan well into the 1960s, but external factors would change all of that.

Leyland's acquisition of AEC was just the first step towards creating the monster that became British Leyland. Leyland bought into Bristol and Eastern Coach Works in 1965, and in 1968 acquired British Motor Holdings – essentially a significant part of the British motor industry, which included Daimler and Guy. With a mixed inheritance of models it made sense to rationalise the Leyland bus range, and any difficult decisions were made easier by the impending Transport Act that offered bus operators incentives to buy buses suitable for driver-only operation. The New Bus Grants scheme signalled the end of the front-engined double-deck chassis and so Leyland entered the 1970s with three double-deck models – the Atlantean, the Fleetline and Bristol's new VRT – and to some at Leyland that was two too many.

One of the first independent operators to take delivery of an Atlantean was Silver Star of Porton Down, which received one a year between 1959 and 1962, all with Weymann semi-lowheight bodies. This was the last one, seen in preservation in 1993. *Tony Wilson*

Above: The Ribble 'Gay Hostess' double-deck coaches were based on a standard Weymann-built shell and PDR1/1 Atlantean chassis fitted with the beefier O. 680 engine. This example was delivered to Ribble in 1960 and was working for its Standerwick subsidiary when photographed in 1965. It had seats for 50 passengers, with toilet and luggage accommodation at the rear of the lower deck. *Ted Jones*

Above right: Belfast Corporation tried an early Atlantean and went on to buy another three in 1964. This was the 1960 PDR1/1 with Alexander 77-seat body, but Belfast's next Atlanteans had locally built MH Coachworks bodies. *Howard Cunningham*

To allay fears about the manoeuvrability of the Atlantean, Leyland released drawings showing that a 29ft 9in-long Atlantean had a swept turning circle no greater than a shorter (26ft 11in) Titan PD2.

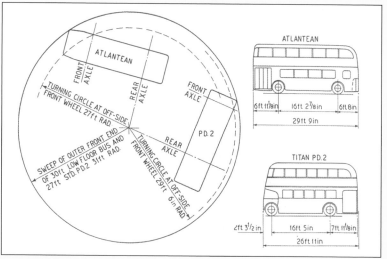

Improvements and new variations

Early Atlanteans were not without their problems. There were tales of chassis flexing and even cracking under the weight of the 'power pack' at the rear, problems with the braking system in cold weather, and strain on the clutch and gearbox from the extra weight and heavy use. Drivers were remote from the engine and were unable to hear noises that would have alerted them to problems. The engine cooling and saloon heating systems were temperamental and fuel consumption was high.

With around 1,500 Atlanteans in service, Leyland moved to address these problems and following discussions with operators, the chassis was strengthened. Although Leyland had made much of the

Leicester City Transport took three of these 77-seat Metro-Cammell-bodied PDR1/1s in 1962, returning for more Atlanteans in 1968/69, this time with ECW and Park Royal bodies. *Geoffrey Morant*

Bolton Corporation bought its first Atlanteans in 1963 and went on to build up a fleet of over a hundred during the next seven years until the undertaking was subsumed by SELNEC PTE. This is a 1968 PDR1/1 with East Lancs 78-seat bodywork, seen in 1969. *Ted Jones*

Portsmouth Corporation bought more than 150 Atlanteans over 18 years, including some rare single-deckers. This 1966 PDR1/1 has Metro-Cammell 76-seat bodywork to the style first introduced in 1958. *Ted Jones*

The last Atlanteans delivered to Salford Corporation, in 1969, were PDR1A/1s with two-door 72-seat Park Royal bodies like this one seen in 1972 in SELNEC PTE ownership. Twenty Atlanteans on order at the time the PTE was created were delivered to SELNEC with Manchester-style Mancunian bodies. *Kevin Lane*

ease and speed with which the engine and gearbox could be removed for maintenance, engineers realised that they would prefer not to remove these units but to work on them in place. So, in 1963, the Atlantean MkII was introduced, with modifications that made gearbox removal easier, a three-piece engine cover for easier access, a beefed-up O.600 engine and a fluid friction rather than centrifugal clutch.

These changes attracted new customers and in 1963 the Atlantean was, for the first time, the UK's best-selling double-decker. Atlantean converts in 1962/63 included the Bolton, Bury, Leicester, Portsmouth and Salford municipal fleets, and a growing number of independent operators – Bamber Bridge Motor Services, J Fishwick & Sons, Graham's Bus Service and South Yorkshire Motors – most of whom became good repeat customers for the Atlantean. In 1961, Leyland had sold 10 Atlanteans to Birmingham City Transport and no doubt hoped for substantial sales from an important operator that was ready to update its substantial fleet. But unfortunately for Leyland, Birmingham would buy no more new Atlanteans and would turn enthusiastically to the locally built Daimler Fleetline.

John Fishwick & Sons, the Leyland-based independent operator, was a natural home for locally built Leyland products. This is a 1964 PDR1/1 with Weymann 73-seat semi-lowheight bodywork. *Stewart J Brown*

Pontefract-based independent South Yorkshire Motors operated this 1971 PDR1/3 Atlantean with Northern Counties 70-seat body. *Stewart J Brown*

Birmingham City Transport, one of Britain's largest bus fleets, was a prime target for the Atlantean, and Leyland delivered 10 PDR1/1s in 1961 with 76-seat Metro-Cammell bodies. Birmingham also bought a former Leyland demonstrator that had worked in the city. These would be Birmingham's last Atlanteans, however, as it standardised on the Daimler Fleetline for the rest of its existence as a municipal operator. Its successor, West Midlands PTE, continued to buy Fleetlines. *Arnold Richardson*

Below: An order from Coventry, home of Daimler, seemed like a coup for Leyland, but the 20 PDR1/2s with Willowbrook 76-seat bodies delivered to the corporation in 1964 would prove to be Coventry's only Atlanteans as it turned to the Daimler Fleetline. The Coventry buses were the first deliveries of the new lowheight PDR1/2 chassis, although the bodies were built to normal height. *Roy Marshall*

Concerned by the success of the Fleetline, which by 1964 was actually outselling the Atlantean, Leyland developed its own Fleetline substitute. This was the Atlantean PDR1/2 using the drop-centre rear axle from the Leyland-Albion Lowlander, a lowheight front-engined model developed with Scottish Bus Group sales in mind. The PDR1/2 also used a gearbox similar to the Daimler unit on the Fleetline, and now Leyland could offer a true lowheight model to replace the awkward semi-lowheight version; the last of 344 of these were delivered in 1966.

The first PDR1/2 Atlanteans in service were, ironically, for Coventry Corporation, which received 22 in 1964. Although this gave the operator the chance to compare them with Coventry-built Fleetlines, no more Atlanteans would join the fleet. Some Leyland customers moved to the PDR1/2 to accommodate lowheight bodies, while others specified normal-height bodies.

More bodybuilders were now building on the Atlantean chassis. In 1963/64, East Lancs, Neepsend, Northern Counties, Park Royal and Willowbrook all built on the chassis for the first time. And after the bland body styles offered in the early years there was a backlash from some customers who wanted distinctively styled bodies, resurrecting a trend that meant that Birmingham, Glasgow, Leeds, Liverpool and Manchester buses were often instantly recognisable.

BET companies tended to be content with the bodybuilders' standard products, but the larger municipalities looked for something different. While the bodies for rear-engined double-deckers developed for Birmingham and Manchester were essentially tweaked versions of a standard shape, Bolton, Glasgow and Liverpool worked with their suppliers to come up with designs that made a much more positive statement on the streets.

The Alexander bodies for Glasgow from 1962 onwards took advantage of changes in legislation that permitted non-opening windscreens, and Alexander made much use of fibreglass to give the buses a more rounded appearance. Liverpool and Metro-Cammell went for a more angular but equally striking look, the Liverpool buses having a longer wheelbase – 16ft 9in (5.11m) rather than the normal 16ft 3in (4.95m) of other PDR1 models. The Irish state-owned bus operator, Córas Iompair Éireann (CIÉ), also opted for the longer wheelbase on its PDR1 fleet.

While the 'Glasgow' design became Alexander's standard product, Metro-Cammell continued to offer its more conventional bodies. Bolton and East Lancs came up with a design that combined deep windows, a peaked dome and a faired-in engine compartment with a more contemporary livery application, which almost certainly influenced later designs.

The 'notch' at the back between the upper deck and the 'power pack', to allow the engine cover to be raised, was a distinctive feature of most early Atlanteans, but operators wanting a cleaner-looking side elevation specified shrouds that disguised the shape but still allowed access to the mechanical units.

The drop-centre rear axle that allowed the PDR1/2 Atlantean to be a true lowheight bus in the same mould as Daimler's Fleetline.

New customers

Atlantean sales, dented by the arrival of the Fleetline, picked up in the mid-1960s, so much so that Leyland sold more than 500 into the UK market in 1966, only to lose out in sales to Daimler in 1967. The two manufacturers ran neck and neck during the late 1960s, but the Fleetline outsold the Atlantean in the period 1964-69 by around 6%.

New Atlantean customers in the mid-1960s were municipals like Ashton, Bournemouth, Edinburgh, Leeds, Lincoln, Maidstone, Newport, Nottingham, Oldham and Stockton, as well as independents like AA Motor Services, A1 Service, Delaine Coaches, West Riding Automobile and Whippet Coaches, and interesting customers like British Overseas Airways Corporation (BOAC) and London Transport. A couple of 'firsts' at the time: Massey bodied its first Atlanteans, and Great Yarmouth received short-length 28ft (8.5m) PDR1/2s.

The LT order was particularly interesting. In 1965, LT was still receiving deliveries of its Routemaster model and would do so until 1968, but it was also looking at a range of alternatives that included

There was a flood of new Atlantean customers in the mid-1960s, some of whom would turn out to be regular customers while others would disappear when the PTEs were created. Ashton-under-Lyne Corporation was absorbed by SELNEC PTE in 1969, but not before it had bought batches of the Atlantean in 1966 and 1969, and buses that had been ordered by Ashton were delivered to SELNEC, including six that became the prototypes of SELNEC's new standard double-decker. This is one of five Ashton PDR1A/1 Atlanteans with 71-seat Northern Counties two-door bodywork delivered in 1969, seen when new. *Geoffrey Morant*

Bournemouth Corporation was a good customer for the PDR-series Atlantean, though it moved to the Daimler Fleetline in the 1970s. These PDR1A/1 Atlanteans, seen in 1979, are an Alexander-bodied 1971 example on the left passing a 1966 Weymann-bodied bus. The Weymann body has a front end that echoes Alexander practice. *Gavin Booth*

Below: Oldham Corporation bought its first Atlanteans in 1965, following batches of the Leyland Titan. This is a 1966-delivered PDR1A/1 with 77-seat East Lancs body, seen when new. Later Atlanteans ordered by Oldham would be delivered directly to the new SELNEC PTE. *Geoffrey Morant*

rear-engined double-deckers as well as standee single-deckers. It took 50 Atlantean PDR1/1s with O.680 engines and 72-seat bodies, and although some more stylish designs were available it went for a conventional-looking Park Royal body. At the same time it received eight Daimler Fleetlines with similar bodies. The Atlanteans proved troublesome, so in 1973 they were sold for further service in Hong Kong. The Fleetlines were more successful and led to substantial orders, but as it turned out, most of them were withdrawn prematurely.

Right: Alexander-bodied Atlanteans like this 1968 PDR1/1, seen in 1976, were bought by Newport Transport between 1966 and 1971, after which the undertaking switched to Scania/MCW single-deck and double-deck models. *Sholto Thomas*

Maidstone Corporation bought Atlanteans between 1965 and 1972 with bodywork built in Wigan by Massey and, as here, by Northern Counties on a 1971 PDR1A/1 74-seater, seen in 1973.
Stewart J Brown

Above: Stockton Corporation bought Atlanteans in 1964-66, while nearby Middlesbrough Corporation bought Daimler Fleetlines. When the two municipals were merged with the Teesside Railless Traction Board in 1968 as Teesside Municipal Transport (TMT) more Atlanteans were bought, but TMT's successor, Cleveland Transit, became a firm Fleetline fan. This 1966 ex-Stockton PDR1/1 Atlantean, seen in Middlesbrough in Cleveland days, has 74-seat Park Royal bodywork to a design that would influence LT's 50 Atlanteans. *Tony Wilson*

More independent operators turned to the Atlantean in the mid-1960s. The various members of the A1 Service co-operative in Ayrshire bought some 25 PDR1 and AN68 Atlanteans over a number of years. This 1968 PDR1/1 was one of A1 Service's first and has a Nottingham-style Northern Counties 77-seat body. It is seen in Ardrossan in 1973. A1 Service members also bought 37 Fleetlines. *Gavin Booth*

Above: After it had invested in several significant batches of Guy's advanced front-engined Wulfrunian in the early 1960s the independent West Riding company ordered 25 Atlantean PDR1/2s with lowheight Roe 76-seat bodies in 1966. One of these is seen in Leeds in National Bus Company red in 1978. West Riding was sold to the Transport Holding Company in 1967 and passed into the new NBC in 1969. *Sholto Thomas*

BOAC bought 15 coach-seated PDR1/1 Atlanteans with Metro-Cammell bodies in 1966, and a further six PDR2/1s with Leeds-style Roe 65-seat bodies in 1971. One of the later vehicles is seen on the M4 near Hayes on its normal duties when photographed in 1978 in British Airways livery, transferring airline passengers between central London and Heathrow Airport. In 1972, the businesses of BOAC and British European Airways (BEA) were combined under the newly formed British Airways Board, with the separate airlines coming together as British Airways in 1974. *Tony Wilson*

More Leeds-style Roe-bodied PDR2/1 Atlanteans were supplied for airport work to Halls of Hounslow – three in 1969 and five in 1972 – operating on contract to Trans World Airlines between central London and Heathrow. This 1972 example is seen in Trafalgar Square in 1976 on sightseeing duties for London Cityrama.
Gavin Booth

A longer Atlantean chassis was introduced at the 1966 Commercial Vehicle Show, designated PDR2/1. This had the O.680 engine as standard and allowed for 33ft (10m) long bodies. Although initially designated O.680, Leyland soon dropped the 'O' (Oil) prefix and the same engine was now simply designated 680. PDR2/1 deliveries started in 1968 and early customers who would return for further batches included Leeds, Manchester, Plymouth and Sheffield corporations.

There were changes to the standard PDR1/1, which became the PDR1A/1 following the fitting of a rationalised Pneumocyclic gearbox. The PDR1/2 was not affected, and the PDR2/1 had the gearbox fitted as standard. In 1967, after 479 deliveries, the lowheight PDR1/2 chassis became the PDR1/3 with changes to the gearbox and transmission. The PDR1/3 would be a rare Atlantean variant, with just 81 chassis built.

The first single-deck Atlanteans appeared in 1968 – three Marshall-bodied PDR1/1s for Great Yarmouth Corporation – and more single-deck versions appeared in 1971 – PDR2/1s for Portsmouth with Seddon bodies and for Merseyside PTE (ordered by Birkenhead Corporation) with Northern Counties bodies.

More new Atlantean customers in the late 1960s included the Aberdeen, Accrington, Birkenhead, Blackburn, Bradford, Colchester, Ipswich, Southampton, Teesside and Wigan municipal fleets; independents Cunningham's Bus Services, King Alfred Motor Services and South Notts Bus Company; and BET fleets Rhondda, Stratford Blue and Yorkshire Woollen. The Road Transport Industry Training Board bought two PDR2/1s for training purposes, and Halls of Hounslow bought eight for airport transfer work on behalf of Trans World Airlines between London and Heathrow Airport. The BOAC PDR1/1s bought in 1965 were used for similar work from Victoria to Heathrow. Both batches for airline work had coach seating and were capable of higher speeds.

As the 1960s drew to a close, major upheavals in the UK bus industry would have their effect on sales of the Atlantean and its competitors – and the Atlantean itself, in production for more than a decade, was ready for a revamp.

Great Yarmouth Corporation was an early Atlantean customer, in 1960, and went on to specify some of the more unusual variants. Three of these short-length (28ft) PDR1/2s were delivered in 1966 with 65-seat Roe bodies, as seen here in 1979. *Gavin Booth*

Below left and right: Great Yarmouth also bought the first Atlanteans to receive single-deck bodies – three PDR1/1s with 31ft-long Marshall 39-seat bodies. The result was neat, as seen in this 1970 seaside view. The depot view shows the rear-end treatment. *Ted Jones/Tony Wilson*

LT's order for 50 Atlanteans and eight Daimler Fleetlines indicated that it was prepared to look at newer rear-engined double-deck designs while it was still buying more than 300 front-engined Routemasters each year. The Atlanteans and Fleetlines had bodywork by Park Royal based on bodies supplied to Stockton Corporation, even though Park Royal had arguably produced more attractive bodies for other operators. The London Atlanteans had short lives with their original owner and were sold to China Motor Bus, Hong Kong, in 1973. This 1965 Atlantean is seen in Parliament Square, London, in 1968. *Ted Jones*

Below: The much-loved Winchester independent King Alfred Motor Services bought four PDR1/2 Atlanteans with lowheight Roe 76-seat bodies in 1967, and one is seen here in 1973 after the business had been sold to National Bus Company's Hants & Dorset subsidiary. The Atlantean still wears King Alfred colours but carries its new H&D fleet number. Alongside is a 1962 King Alfred Leyland Leopard PSU3/2R with Willowbrook 53-seat bus body. *Tony Wilson*

The BET fleet Stratford Blue received three PDR1A/1 Atlanteans with 75-seat Northern Counties bodies in 1967. The company, a subsidiary of Midland Red, was a staunch Leyland fan and received very few of Midland Red's own-build BMMO vehicles. Stratford Blue was absorbed into its parent fleet in 1971. *Geoffrey Morant*

The Road Transport Industry Training Board bought two of these PDR2/1 Atlanteans with Sheffield-style Park Royal 79-seat dual-door bodywork in 1968. This one is at its training centre at MOTEC, Livingston. *Gavin Booth*

Similar PDR2/1s with Park Royal bodies were bought by Plymouth Corporation in 1968-71. This 1970 example is seen in 1986. *Gavin Booth*

Changes all round

The late 1960s was a period of great change in the UK bus manufacturing and bus operating industries. The juggernaut that was British Leyland had started in the early part of the decade with some sensible acquisitions; it ended up, with more than a little government encouragement, as an unwieldy monster in 1968. With a vast empire – motorcars, vans, trucks, buses and much more – the ailing British car manufacturer received much of the attention and the investment, while the bus business was left to carry on as before.

Now under Leyland's bus umbrella were AEC, Bristol, Daimler, Guy and Leyland itself, as well as the Eastern Coach Works (ECW), Park Royal and Roe bodybuilders. There were competing models from different stables and it made sense to trim the ranges. Following the example of the Atlantean, chassis manufacturers had

seen a future in rear-engined single-deckers for urban work, and AEC, Bristol, Daimler and Leyland all offered models – of varying reliability, it must be said. British Leyland offered just three double-deck models – Daimler's Fleetline, Bristol's still very new VRT, and Leyland's Atlantean, which like the Fleetline had been in production through the 1960s.

National Bus Company's new London Country company, formed from the London Transport Country Area in 1970, bought 120 Atlantean PDR1A/1 Specials in 1972. Most had attractive Park Royal bodies like this early delivery, photographed in Stevenage in 1976. *Tony Wilson*

In 1969-71, the new Merseyside PTE bought 125 Atlantean PDR2/1s with Alexander two-door bodies. In Liverpool in 1974 is a 79-seater, new in 1971.
Tony Wilson

H W Hunter & Sons of Seaton Delaval, operating in the north-east of England, bought this Roe-bodied 72-seat two-door Atlantean PDR1A/1 in 1971. It is seen here in 1978. *Geoffrey Morant*

The improved AN68-series Atlantean attracted new customers to the model. Between 1973 and 1978, Brighton Corporation bought Atlanteans with Willowbrook and, as here, East Lancs bodies. This 1978 AN68A.1R is seen in 1990. *H J Black*

Then there were the changes to the operating industry and the creation of the National Bus Company from the Tilling and BET groups. Tilling had been state owned since 1948, but BET sold out to the state in 1968 and now the two very different organisations, covering much of England and Wales between them, were being welded into one massive business. This in itself was not bad news for Leyland, which supplied most of the chassis and many of the bodies to Tilling and BET and could see that future vehicle policy would surely be in its favour.

Around the same time, the first four Passenger Transport Executives (PTEs) were set up with a wide remit to plan and operate transport services in four conurbations – based on Birmingham, Liverpool, Manchester and Newcastle. All of the municipal operators in these PTE areas disappeared into these new monoliths, but again Leyland could see opportunities as new standard buses were bought to replace the very varied corporation fleets that had been inherited. The need for new buses would also be helped along by the government's New Bus Grants scheme that provided grants of 25%, rising to 50%, to encourage the purchase of new buses suitable for driver-only operation.

To prepare for what it must have anticipated as a golden period for bus sales, Leyland started cutting its overlapping ranges. The front-engined double-deckers had gone by 1970 and the rear-engined single-deckers soon followed. Here there was a good reason: the integral Leyland National urban bus, to be built as a joint venture with National Bus Company (NBC) on production lines in a new factory in Workington. And there were rumblings that Leyland wanted to do something similar with its double-deck range.

Some operators were unhappy about Leyland's virtual monopoly of the UK bus market and encouraged other manufacturers to get involved. Truck builder Seddon and a collaboration between Metro-Cammell and Scania nudged at the single-deck market, but with limited success. Bedford and Ford, best known for coach chassis, sold lightweight bus chassis into fleets of all sizes, but not enough to upset the mighty Leyland.

In 1975, Fylde Borough Transport, the former Lytham St Annes Corporation, bought six AN68.1R Atlanteans with Northern Counties bodies, finished by Willowbrook, hence the badge on the front panel. *Gavin Booth*

West Yorkshire PTE-style 77-seat Roe bodywork was provided for independent operators requiring small batches of Atlanteans. W Gash & Sons of Newark bought just one new Atlantean, this 1979 AN68A.1R, seen in 1985. *Geoffrey Morant*

The three double-deck chassis were safe for the moment, and three of the new PTEs were customers for the Atlantean – Merseyside, Tyneside and SELNEC (covering Greater Manchester). They all started buying Atlanteans in 1969, including some that had been ordered by their constituent fleets, and started to develop standard designs. Manchester Corporation had introduced a striking new double-decker, the Mancunian, in 1968 – a stylish and undoubtedly modern boxy shape carrying a brighter livery. It had two doors – providing a separate entrance and exit – a layout that was being specified by many operators at the time. While deliveries of the Mancunian continued under SELNEC, the PTE was developing a new standard double-decker that would be built by the hundred.

The number of new operators buying Atlanteans was dropping, but in 1970-72 these included Brighton, Eastbourne and Lytham St Annes corporations, and the independents Garelochhead Coach Services, H W Hunter & Sons and Weardale Motor Services. An important new customer was London Country Bus Services, an NBC company formed out of the London Transport Country Area in 1970, which bought 120 Atlanteans in 1972 to replace ageing AEC Regent RTs inherited from LT.

F Procter & Son of Hanley took delivery of two Atlantean AN68.1Rs in 1974 with Glasgow-style Alexander 76-seat bodywork, as seen in 1977. *Geoffrey Morant*

Blackpool Transport was a late convert to the Atlantean, buying Leyland Titan PD3s until 1968, followed by batches of AEC Swift single-deckers during the early 1970s. This Atlantean AN68A.2R with East Lancs 86-seat body is seen when new in 1980. *Gavin Booth*

As it entered the 1970s, Leyland was looking hard at its inherited model range. There was duplication in its urban rear-engined single-deck models, all introduced in the 1960s, and, as we have seen, these would soon disappear from the model lists, at least for home market customers. Leyland's agenda here was driven by the imminent appearance of the integral Leyland National bus.

Grampian Regional Transport standardised on the Atlantean from 1973 to 1983, all with Alexander bodywork. This 1980 AN68A.1R is seen when new. *Gavin Booth*

There were just the three double-deck models left, all rear-engined following the purge of the front-engined types. The Atlantean and Daimler Fleetline were well established, but Bristol's VRT was a much newer product. The Atlantean was showing its age, and Leyland started an exercise that would result in the AN68 range, which replaced the PDR range.

There were two right-hand drive models, the AN68.1R and AN68.2R – Leyland had changed its chassis designations to dots – but before these were launched in 1972, there were some crossover PDR1A/1 Special models incorporating much of the AN68 specification. There were 120 for London Country and 20 for Maidstone & District, its first new Atlanteans since 1963. Left-hand drive PDR1 Atlanteans had been coded LPDR1, but

The combination of Atlantean chassis and East Lancs bodywork became a favourite with municipal operators in several parts of England. Blackburn, home of East Lancs, was an obvious customer, and this is a 1975 AN68.1R with 76-seat body in Accrington in 1984. *H J Black*

Accrington Corporation (Hyndburn Transport after local government reorganisation) also bought East Lancs-bodied Atlanteans like this 1972 AN68.1R with 72-seat body, seen in Accrington in 1984. *H J Black*

the AN68 versions were AN68.2L etc. The prototype AN68.2R chassis was built in 1970 and bodied by Alexander as a development vehicle for the orders that would materialise from Baghdad and Tehran. In 1980, fitted with the turbocharged 690 engine, it was sold to J Rennie of Dunfermline.

The AN68 featured the 680 engine and its specification reflected the lessons learnt from 14 years of working Atlanteans. The AN68.1R was 30ft 10in (9.40m) long and the AN68/2R was 33ft (10m). There was no lowheight equivalent of the PDR1/3 as the Fleetline and VRT accommodated lowheight bodies, and from 1970 Leyland had offered its 680 engine in the Fleetline as an alternative to the Gardner 6LXB.

Rossendale Transport was another municipal company in the north-west of England that favoured East Lancs-bodied Atlanteans. Seen in 1982, this is a 1977 AN68A.1R with 75-seat body. *Gavin Booth*

Warrington Borough Transport also bought East Lancs-bodied Atlanteans. This 1981 AN68B.1R, seen in 1984, is a 76-seater. *Gavin Booth*

Lothian Region Transport, formerly Edinburgh Corporation, had standardised on Atlanteans from 1966 until 1981 and at one stage had an all-Atlantean double-deck fleet. This 1979 AN68A.1R with Alexander 75-seat two-door body is seen in 1996. Edinburgh pioneered the use of double-deckers with panoramic side windows and continued to specify these for its Atlanteans to the end. *Gavin Booth*

Although the National Bus Company's favoured double-deck model in the 1970s was the Bristol VRT, the demand for new buses under the New Bus Grant scheme caused NBC to turn to Leyland for AN68 Atlanteans, and these carried bodies by Leyland's 'in-house' builders, Eastern Coach Works, Park Royal and Roe. This is a 1976 Ribble AN68.1R with 73-seat Park Royal body at Grasmere in 1984. *Gavin Booth*

Roe also built bodywork to the Park Royal design, as on this 1975 Southdown AN68.1R 73-seater, seen in Portsmouth in 1977, where it was vying for attention with The New Seekers, The Wurzels, Pam Ayres and Bobby Crush. Southdown had spurned the Atlantean for the Titan PD3 during the 1960s. *Sholto Thomas*

Production of the AN68 started in 1972 and would continue for more than a decade. The first customers included a significant number of Atlantean faithfuls, and these were joined by new customers, attracted perhaps by tales of the improved performance of the model. New municipal customers during the 1970s (including some existing Atlantean users that gained new names in the mid-1970s at the time of local government reorganisation) included Blackpool, Caerphilly UDC, East Staffordshire (Burton on Trent), Fylde (Lytham St Annes), Grampian (Aberdeen), Hyndburn (Accrington), Lothian (Edinburgh), Preston, Rhymney Valley (Bedwas & Machen, Caerphilly, Gelligaer), Rossendale (Haslingden, Rawtenstall), Southport and Warrington. It is interesting that late Atlantean converts like Blackpool, Preston, Rossendale, Southport and Warrington were all in north-west England and virtually on Leyland's doorstep. New independent customers were W Gash & Sons, A Hornsby, C S Pegg and F Procter & Son; new NBC fleets were East Kent, Midland General and Southdown – Southdown had stayed firmly with Titan PD3s as long as it could.

Other NBC fleets that received AN68s were established Atlantean customers like London Country, Northern General, Ribble, Trent and Yorkshire Woollen, all companies that were probably glad to get Leyland double-deckers when the standard NBC offering was the Bristol VRT. The Atlanteans were initially ordered to speed deliveries when the New Bus Grants scheme was encouraging operators to invest. Deliveries with Park Royal and Roe bodies started in 1973, but by the time the last NBC Atlanteans were delivered in 1981, they carried either ECW or Roe bodies – both bodybuilders within Leyland Bus. Park Royal had closed in 1980.

Ulsterbus bought its first Atlanteans in 1971 and received 40 with Alexander (Belfast) bodies over the next two years. These were PDR2/1 rather than AN68.2R models. Another new customer was Citybus in Northern Ireland. Its predecessor, Belfast Corporation, had bought an early Atlantean/Alexander in 1960 and three more in 1964 with locally built bodywork. In 1975/76, Citybus received 40 AN68.2Rs with Alexander (Belfast) bodies.

The NBC Atlanteans went to former BET Group fleets, most with a Leyland, if not Atlantean, pedigree. This 1974 East Yorkshire AN68.1R with Park Royal 73-seat body is at North Frodingham in 1979. *Tony Wilson*

Deliveries of Atlanteans to NBC companies continued until 1981, with bodywork on later orders built by ECW or Roe following the decision to close Park Royal in 1980. This 1979 AN68A.1R for Yorkshire Woollen with 74-seat ECW bodywork is seen in Dewsbury in 1981. *H J Black*

A 1980 Northern General AN68A.1R with 73-seat Roe body is pictured in Newcastle's Northumberland Street in 1981 before this area was pedestrianised. The yellow livery was NBC's concession to Tyne & Wear PTE for its buses running in the PTE area. *Gavin Booth*

In 1975/76, Citybus in Belfast received 40 Atlantean AN68.2Rs with Alexander (Belfast) 86-seat bodies. One of these is seen in the city in 1979. *Raymond Bell*

Ulsterbus took 40 late-model PDR2/1 Atlanteans between 1971 and 1973 with 85-seat Alexander (Belfast) bodies. This one is brand new on delivery at Duncrue Street, Belfast, in 1971. *Howard Cunningham*

Weardale Motor Services of Stanhope bought its only new Atlantean, this PDR2/1 with Leeds-style Roe 78-seat body, in 1970. It is seen at Stanhope in 1990. Weardale had a tradition of obtaining registration marks with the figure '6'. *John Young*

Probably the most important group of customers were the new PTEs. The first four – Merseyside, SELNEC, Tyneside and West Midlands – had been set up at the end of the 1960s, and some would undergo name changes as their areas of responsibility increased; SELNEC became Greater Manchester and Tyneside became Tyne & Wear. Then, in the 1970s, new PTEs were created at Greater Glasgow (later Strathclyde), West Yorkshire and South Yorkshire. All of the PTEs except West Midlands became important Atlantean AN68 customers, some right to the end of production.

Looking to the future

The early 1970s was a period of industrial unrest, which caused problems in the supply of chassis as well as engines and other components and resulted in delays at bodybuilders as chassis regularly arrived late. In 1973, Fleetline chassis production was transferred from Coventry to the Leyland factory in Lancashire and this caused serious production delays.

But Leyland needed to look to the double-decker of the future, particularly in the light of new competitors that had appeared on the scene in 1973. The Scania/MCW Metropolitan was a Swedish take on double-deck design, and the Ailsa was a very different animal – a front-engined bus with Volvo running units. Both models were bought by all of the PTEs and London Transport, which must have caused mild panic at Leyland. Although the quantities were small in some cases, Tyne & Wear PTE and London Transport took 144 and 164 Metropolitans respectively, and Greater Glasgow went on to build up a fleet of 137 Ailsas. South Yorkshire and West Midlands PTEs also took significant batches of Ailsas.

There would be other rival double-deck models, notably the Dennis Dominator in 1977 and the MCW Metrobus in 1979, both designed to tap into the Fleetline market. The Dominator became the standard model for South Yorkshire PTE, which bought more than 400, and the Metrobus went on to even greater things in its 10-year production run, notably with London Transport and West Midlands PTE. But in a way these came too late to damage Atlantean sales, which were mainly to existing customers with the bonus of a late surge of export business, including some substantial new customers.

Some Atlantean customers sampled other types, like Southampton City Transport, which tried both the Dennis Dominator and Leyland Olympian before turning to single-deckers in a big way. This is a 1984 Olympian with 76-seat East Lancs body in 1991 in the company of a 1978 Atlantean AN68A.1R also with 76-seat East Lancs body. *Gavin Booth*

Although Greater Manchester PTE had largely standardised on Atlanteans and Fleetlines through the 1970s and early 1980s, it also tried batches of other double-deck types that came on to the market, like the Bristol VRT, Dennis Dominator, Foden-NC, MCW Metrobus, Scania/MCW Metropolitan and Volvo Ailsa. In Oldham in 1988, passengers board a 1983 Atlantean AN68D.1R with Northern Counties 75-seat body, with, behind, a 1982 MCW Metrobus 73-seater, from substantial batches bought between 1979 and 1987. *Gavin Booth*

Leyland had known for some time that a new double-deck model was needed. It was already understood that the Fleetline would be the first of the Leyland models to go, and the last were built in 1980. The Bristol VRT would linger until 1981, but the Atlantean would survive until 1984.

Leyland's thinking was epitomised by its approach to the single-deck bus market – eliminating any competing chassis on its model list to concentrate on one standard integral product, the National. And it looked for a while that its double-deck range would go the same way. Its B15 project vehicle was unveiled in 1975 – an advanced full-height integral double-decker – but when it went into production as the Titan in 1978/79 it was beset by labour problems. The first Titans were to be built at the Park Royal factory in London, and then transferred to AEC at Southall in a joint venture with LT and NBC. However, the AEC move never happened as the factory was closed, as was the Park Royal works, though only after 250 Titans had been built. The next possible home was ECW at Lowestoft, but this move also failed to materialise and production transferred to the Leyland National Workington site in Cumbria. By this time, many operators had cancelled or reduced orders and the Titan became essentially a London bus – admittedly a successful one.

This did not help Leyland's dilemma, so its B45 project was launched at the Bristol factory, emerging in 1980 as the hugely successful Olympian, which many customers regarded as a worthy successor to the Atlantean.

Greater Manchester was also one of the handful of operators to take delivery of Leyland's advanced Titan TN15 model. A 1980-delivered 73-seater sits at Stockport in 1980 with Atlanteans in the background. Although GM had ordered 50 Titans, only 15 were delivered.
Gavin Booth

Below: Newcastle Corporation and Tyne & Wear PTE buses at the Dunbar Rally in 1982 illustrate the development of rear-engined double-deckers and Alexander body styles. On the left is the preserved 1962 PDR1/1 Atlantean, in the centre a 1981 AN68A.2R 78-seater, and on the right one of two newly delivered 78-seat Scania BR112DRs.
Gavin Booth

Borrowed time

The Atlantean was now living on borrowed time. New European legislation on engine noise was taking effect on vehicles registered after 1 April 1983, and it was known that the Atlantean would not meet this. Leyland was given a 12-month dispensation to allow the last chassis to be built and bodied. Even so, new customers kept turning up and existing customers came back for more, right up to the very end.

There had been changes to the specification that altered the chassis designations. So the 1975 AN68A featured Leyland's new G2 gearbox and power steering as standard on all models; the 1979 AN68B had a Friedmann & Maier fuel pump and air-operated accelerator; the 1980 AN68C reverted to the semi-automatic gearbox as standard; and the 1982 AN68D had a rationalised version of the 680 engine.

J J Longstaff & Sons of Mirfield was a late customer for the Atlantean, buying its only new example in 1982, an AN68C.2R with Northern Counties 83-seat body, seen here leaving Dewsbury bus station in 1983. *H J Black*

Another new customer was Limebourne of London, which bought this AN68.1R with West Yorkshire PTE-style Roe 75-seat body in 1980 for Cityrama sightseeing work. It is seen at Victoria in 1981 in the company of an LT MCW Metrobus working on the recently introduced Airbus A1 service. *Gavin Booth*

Similar Roe 77-seat bodywork was fitted to this 1979 AN68A.1R for Harold Wilson Ltd (Premier) of Stainforth, seen when new in Doncaster. *Gavin Booth*

Lancaster City Transport bought its first Atlanteans, East Lancs 86-seat AN68D.2R models, in 1982. One is seen at Morecambe in 1983. *Gavin Booth*

Below: Barrow Corporation was the last new home market customer for the Atlantean, taking four AN68D.1Rs with 75-seat Northern Counties bodies in 1983/84. *Sholto Thomas*

Greater Manchester continued to add to its massive Atlantean fleet until 1984. This is a 1983 AN68D.1R with 75-seat Northern Counties body, turning into Piccadilly, Manchester, in 1988. Its external vinyls promote GM Buses in an age of intense local competition. *Gavin Booth*

Kingston upon Hull City Transport built up a significant Atlantean fleet between 1960 and 1982. This is one of its final deliveries, a 1982 AN68C.1R with 74-seat Roe body, seen in 1992. *Gavin Booth*

The Greater Manchester Atlanteans sold in 1986 were bought by operators throughout Britain, including relatively local fleets like Hyndburn Transport. This 1975 AN68A.1R/Northern Counties is seen in Accrington in 1988. *Gavin Booth*

Below: Some of the Greater Manchester Atlanteans were used in competition with their former owner, like this somewhat battered 1975 AN68.1R/Northern Counties working for Bee Line in Piccadilly, Manchester, in 1990. It had come via the London Country fleet, as can be detected under the hastily applied vinyls. *Gavin Booth*

Some of the Manchester Atlanteans were bought by Ribble and survived into Stagecoach ownership of that company. This 1975 AN68A.1R/Northern Counties is seen in 1992. *Gavin Booth*

Greater Manchester Atlanteans could even be found in the Strathclyde Buses fleet, loaned by Western Scottish to cover the disastrous fire at Strathclyde's Larkfield Garage in 1992, which destroyed some 60 buses. This 1978 Park Royal-bodied AN68A.1R is followed by an Alexander-bodied Atlantean borrowed from Grampian. *Gavin Booth*

Preston Bus continued to operate Atlanteans into the 21st century. This is one of its last deliveries, a 1983 AN68D.1R with 86-seat East Lancs body, in Preston's iconic bus station in 2005. *Gavin Booth*

In its last few years on the UK market, the Atlantean continued to sell in substantial numbers to the PTE fleets at Greater Glasgow/Strathclyde, Greater Manchester and Merseyside, as well as to important municipal customers like Grampian, Hull, Lothian, Nottingham, Portsmouth and Southampton, and to NBC fleets like London Country, Northern General and Ribble. New converts to the Atlantean in its final years included some of the municipals in the north-west of England that had resisted its appeal, the last being Barrow, which bought the first of its four Atlanteans in 1983.

And so the last domestic chassis, for Merseyside PTE, rolled off the line at the Farington plant at Leyland in 1984, although export Atlanteans would continue to be built until 1986. In 26 years of production, more than 15,000 Atlantean chassis had been built, and just under two-thirds of these (9,000-plus) were AN68 variants.

When the British bus industry outside London was deregulated in 1986, the appearance of new bus companies wanting to compete with the incumbent operators led to a rush of interest in minibuses and a demand for decent second-hand full-size buses. Greater Manchester Transport prematurely withdrew 450 buses, including 129 Atlanteans and 246 Fleetlines, which were quickly snapped up by operators throughout Britain, including some that used them to compete with GM Buses in Greater Manchester.

The Atlanteans bought by West Yorkshire PTE also lingered into the new century under the ownership of FirstBus. This 1981 AN68C.1R with 75-seat Roe body is seen in Leeds in 2001. *Gavin Booth*

The AN68 had cemented the Atlantean's reputation as a good, reliable, hard-working chassis and some were still in daily service into the 21st century. While many had found second and even third homes, others were still working with their original owners. The last former Ribble Atlanteans ran in 2001 with the companies that had acquired parts of the Ribble business. There were still Atlanteans with other fleets in north-west England – like Blackburn, Blackpool, First Manchester, Fishwick, Merseyside and Preston – though not for much longer. Lothian's last Atlanteans ran in 2000, and there were outposts like Southampton where they kept going for some years beyond that. All three of the big bus groups to emerge after deregulation and privatisation in the 1980s – Arriva, First and Stagecoach – inherited Atlanteans.

Export success

Right from its earliest days, Leyland had recognised the importance of export markets for its products. Its first exports, in 1906, were double-deck buses for use in Bombay, India, and for nearly 90 years, until Volvo dispensed with the Leyland name, many thousands of buses were exported – some as chassis, some with body kits for local assembly, and some with UK-built bodies. Most, inevitably, were single-deckers, but there were thousands of double-deckers too for export markets as near to Lancashire as the Irish Republic and as far away as Indonesia and Australia.

In the years before the Atlantean, Leyland Titans were being shipped over to Commonwealth countries like Australia, Ceylon, India, Kenya, Pakistan, South Africa and Uganda as well as to less obvious markets like Cuba, Denmark and Spain. And Córas Iompair Éireann (CIÉ) in Ireland was a major customer for Leyland products.

With the arrival of the Atlantean, Leyland recognised the importance of giving export customers the opportunity to try the new chassis. Two demonstrators with Metro-Cammell bodies were produced for South Africa in 1960, one each for City Tramways in Cape Town and the Pretoria municipal fleet, and although export orders were slow to materialise, there were locally bodied Atlanteans for Bombay and Delhi in 1962/63, and 12 Busaf-bodied examples in 1965 for Pretoria, which became a regular customer.

South Africa was an early target export customer for the Atlantean, the Pretoria municipal fleet taking examples from 1960. This is a 1968 PDR1/1 with 74-seat bodywork by Bus Bodies (SA) that was clearly influenced by Metro-Cammell designs. *Stewart J Brown*

A less predictable Atlantean customer was Stockholm, which came to Leyland and Park Royal for 200 Panther rear-engined single-deckers and 50 Atlanteans to help with its switch-over to the right-hand rule of the road in 1967. The Atlanteans were 36ft 4½in (11.1m) long and featured front-mounted radiators They were fitted with Voith fully automatic gearboxes, an increasingly popular option in Europe. A Glasgow Atlantean had been fitted with a Voith in 1966, and South Yorkshire PTE would specify Voith boxes in future Atlantean deliveries.

The larger Portuguese cities had been buying British-built double-deckers since World War 2 but these were mainly AECs. Porto went to Leyland for Atlanteans with a batch of 10 in 1962, fitted with bodies built under MCW licence by local firm Martins & Caetano, followed by 30 with Dalfa bodies in 1963/64, and 90 with 680 engines and 32ft 7in (9.93m) Salvador Caetano bodies in 1966, again with front-mounted radiators. A group of four Portuguese independent operators providing services into Lisbon across the new road bridge over the River Tagus bought 36 Atlanteans with bodies built by UTIC between 1968 and 1972.

The 50 Park Royal-bodied Atlanteans delivered to Stockholm in 1967 were impressive buses at 36ft 4½in (11. 1m) long; they had twin staircases and seats for 73 passengers. At the same time Stockholm received 200 Leyland Panthers with Park Royal bodies.

Portuguese independent operators bought 36 Atlantean LPDR1/1s with UTIC 87-seat bodies. This is one of 15 for Transul, seen at Setúbal in 1973. *Dale Tringham*

CIÉ later bought AN68.1R Atlanteans with square-built Van Hool McArdle bodies. This 1975 example is seen in Dublin Bus livery in 1989, passing the Bank of Ireland in the city. *Gavin Booth*

Opposite top: The 90 Atlantean LPDR1/1s for Porto in 1966 had attractive Salvador Caetano 87-seat bodies. *Gavin Booth*

Opposite bottom: The first Atlanteans for CIÉ were PDR1/1 types with Metsec/CIÉ bodies. Seen in O'Connell Street, Dublin, in 1980 are a 1967 78-seater and a 1969 two-door 74-seater. *Gavin Booth*

CIÉ had standardised on the Leyland Titan since 1937 and bought its last, PD3s, in 1961. It turned to the Atlantean in 1966, and over the next eight years bought 602 PDR1/1s with Metsec/CIÉ bodies – although the last 80 are also recorded as Van Hool McArdle bodies, following the partnership between Van Hool and Thomas McArdle Ltd that took over the Spa Road body works in 1973. From 1974, CIÉ turned to the AN68.1R with Van Hool McArdle bodies, and bought 238 until 1977, but suffered mechanical and parts supply problems and retro-fitted DAF engines to many of them. Unhappy with Leyland, CIÉ turned to FFG in Hamburg to design a new range of buses to be built in Ireland, including a double-decker, but these proved equally unsatisfactory and CIÉ later turned back to Leyland for deliveries of the Olympian.

Between 1970 and 1972, the Department for Government Transport in New South Wales received 224 Atlantean PDR1A/1 for service in Sydney, with 66-seat bodies by Pressed Metal Corporation, a subsidiary of Leyland Australia. *John Ward*

The New South Wales Department of Government Transport (DGT) in Sydney, Australia, bought its first Atlanteans in 1970, the start of a fleet that would total 224. There should have been more, but industrial unrest over driver-only operation, as well as reliability problems, caused the balance of 76 of an order for 300 to materialise as single-deck Leopards. After the Atlanteans, DGT turned to articulated buses for its high-capacity needs.

Other export double-deck markets had been firmly in AEC's hands – large fleets of Regent Vs had been built by AEC and Park Royal for Baghdad, Iraq, and Tehran, Iran, but with the removal of the Regent V from the British Leyland model lists the Leyland sales team pushed the Atlantean hard and were rewarded with substantial orders, first from Tehran Omnibus Board, which built up a fleet of over 700 AN68.2Ls between 1972 and 1978, and from PTS,

Baghdad, which took 500 similar buses between 1975 and 1981. The bodies for the Tehran buses were Park Royal kits delivered for local assembly, while the Baghdad buses were delivered complete, half with Park Royal bodies and the rest by Willowbrook following the Park Royal closure; these were built using Park Royal jigs and fittings.

In 1974, two Tehran Atlanteans were diverted to OTCZ to operate in Kinshasa, Zaire, now the Democratic Republic of the Congo, and a Baghdad bus was delivered to Calypso in Gibraltar. Another Baghdad bus was damaged on delivery and passed to Whippet of Fenstanton via a UK dealer. The chassis and Willowbrook body were converted to right-hand drive and the bus was registered by Whippet in 1987. An Iran chassis was sent to Germany where it received a Neoplan body, intended as a demonstrator for Saudi Arabia, but ended up in the UK in non-passenger use.

Baghdad and Tehran became important markets for Atlanteans in the 1970s and early 1980s, with some 1,200 chassis exported. Most of the Baghdad buses had Park Royal bodies like this example, while the similar Park Royal bodies for Tehran were assembled locally from kits.

This Atlantean AN68.2L, pictured in 1992, was delivered to Calypso of Gibraltar in 1989 and is thought to have been built in 1981 as a spare to the last batch of Willowbrook-bodied Atlanteans that went to PTS, Baghdad. The Willowbrook body was built using Park Royal jigs and fittings. *Andy Izatt*

An Iran chassis intended as a demonstrator for Saudi Arabia received a Neoplan body in Germany but ended up in the UK in non-passenger use. *Graham Ashworth*

The New York Metropolitan Transportation Authority ordered eight Atlantean AN68A.2Ls in 1976 with 72-seat Park Royal bodies. One of these is seen at Leyland in 1976 undergoing final preparation before delivery. *Gavin Booth*

One of the New York Atlanteans in service in the city early in 1979. The body style owed much to the Manchester Corporation Mancunian style. Leyland made sure everybody knew who had built these buses. *Gavin Booth*

An unlikely customer in 1976 was the New York Metropolitan Transportation Authority, which ordered eight AN68A.2Ls with Park Royal bodies, but these air-conditioned buses were not greatly successful and in 1980 moved to the west coast to operate in San Francisco while the cable car system was closed for rebuilding.

The New York Atlanteans travelled across the United States to San Francisco in 1980, and this one was still working for Gray Line Tours on Victoria Island, Canada, in 2008. *Royston Morgan*

Singapore Bus Service bought 520 Atlanteans between 1977 and 1986 with bodywork assembled from Alexander, Baco and Metsec or Duple Metsec kits. This is a 1979 delivery, an AN68A.2R with Metsec 85-seat body.

The Far East became an important double-deck market, although operators in Hong Kong, potentially the largest market, chose other double-deck types and only took second-hand Atlanteans, including London's 50 examples. Singapore Bus Service, on the other hand, became an important Atlantean customer, buying more than 500 Atlanteans between 1977 and 1986. These had locally assembled bodies supplied in kit form by Alexander, Baco and Metsec (Duple Metsec from 1981).

A 1986 Singapore Atlantean AN68A.2R with Alexander RHS-type 86-seat body. The Alexander R-type family of bodies was developed for chassis like the Atlantean's successor, the Olympian, so these were the only Atlanteans to carry this body design. *Julian Osborne*

Kuwait ordered 50 Atlantean AN68.2Ls from Leyland, and these received Greater Manchester-style 80-seat Northern Counties bodies. This is a 1979 delivery.

The first left-hand drive Atlanteans bodied by Alexander at Falkirk were 22 AN68.2Ls delivered in 1980 to Metro Manila. Two are shown nearing completion at Falkirk; the rest were assembled in the Philippines. *Gavin Booth*

Late in the Atlantean's life the model was finding new, and often unexpected, export markets. The Kuwait Transport Co, in the Persian Gulf, showed an interest in 1979, and Leyland and Northern Counties built an AN68.2L demonstrator, which was followed by orders in 1980-86 for 50 similar buses. The 1986 deliveries were among the last Atlantean chassis built.

The emphasis then moved to the Far East with orders from the Philippines – 22 AN68.2Ls with Alexander bodies for Metro Manila in 1980; and from Indonesia – over 100 AN68A.2Rs for PPD, Jakarta, in 1980-86, and 31 AN68A.2Rs and AN68D.2Rs with Duple Metsec bodies for DAMRI, Surabaya, in 1981-83, together with 137 similar bodies for the Indonesian government for use in various towns and cities in 1981-83. Many of these chassis were supplied in kit form for local assembly, including the last Atlanteans to be supplied, built in 1986 and shipped to Indonesia in 1987.

Even in the 1980s, when Leyland was pushing its new Olympian as an export model, there were still new markets that preferred the perceived reliability and ruggedness of the Atlantean. In 1983, five AN69.2Ls with Alexander bodies were supplied to Quito in Ecuador.

The AN69 Atlantean used a lightly turbocharged version of its 680 engine, making it quieter and cleaner, and this was specified for some of the later SVAR, Tehran, orders in 1978. The Iranian Revolution in 1979 affected deliveries, and 50 Tehran AN69.2L chassis were converted to right-hand drive, diverted to Pretoria in South Africa, and fitted locally with Busaf bodies.

There were two UK-delivered AN69.2R Atlanteans. As previously mentioned, one was built as a prototype in 1970 and, fitted with a 690 engine, was sold to J Rennie of Dunfermline in 1980. The other had started out as an AN69.2L with Leyland's research department as a prototype of the AN69 series. Converted to right-hand drive and bodied by ECW with a style of body that had been developed for the Leyland Olympian, it entered service with Fishwick, the Leyland-based independent operator, which over the years had received former demonstrators and had in more recent times provided buses that would tour the UK as demonstrators. The existence of a 'tame' operator on Leyland's doorstep was mutually convenient.

One of the Manila Atlanteans in service. Note the conductresses at each door and the 'destination' showing 'Metro Manila', with the actual destination on a board by the front entrance. *BCVM*

Jakarta in Indonesia was another late convert to the Atlantean. This 1981 AN68A.2R with Duple Metsec 85-seat body, operated by the state-owned PPD company, is seen at a busy local bus station in 1984. *Julian Osborne*

Leyland and Alexander supplied five AN69.2L Atlanteans to Quito in 1983. This one was photographed before export to Ecuador.

One of the Quito Atlanteans is seen in service a long way from Leyland and Falkirk, and looking well used. *Julian Osborne*

Opposite top: The Atlantean AN69 was developed as an export model; Leyland used a home market chassis to develop a quiet specification for LT Fleetlines. The chassis received a 74-seat ECW body and was sold to Fishwick of Leyland. *Stewart J Brown*

Opposite bottom: A contrast in Atlantean rears in the Fishwick yard at Leyland. On the left is the 'quiet pack' AN69.1R; next is an ex-Preston AN68A.2R/Alexander; on the right is the AN69.2R with Olympian-style ECW 83-seat body. This had been the prototype AN69.2L and was converted to right-hand drive and bodied by ECW in 1983. *Malcolm Flynn*

The Atlantean assessed

The Atlantean had a good run for Leyland's money. But after 14 years of the PDR series, and almost as long for the better-regarded AN68, the Atlantean had run its course.

In retrospect, it was brave of Leyland to lead the way with such a fundamentally different double-deck design, particularly as it was still relatively untested in 1958 when the first production examples appeared. Although it had gained operating experience with LFDD STF 90 and integral Atlantean 281 ATC, the development of the Atlantean as a chassis in just two years did run the risk that, largely unproven as it was in this form, it could run into problems.

With the creation of the PTEs between 1969 and 1974, Leyland lost many municipal Atlantean customers, although most of the PTEs bought Atlanteans in substantial quantities. Birkenhead Corporation had bought Leyland Titans until 1967, and in 1968/69 bought 28 Atlantean PDR1/2s with Northern Counties bodies. This 1969 71-seater is seen in 1970. Further Atlanteans ordered by Birkenhead were delivered to the new Merseyside PTE. *Dale Tringham*

Above: An early Atlantean customer that built up a large municipal fleet of the model was Sheffield, which latterly favoured the longer PDR2/1 version, although this is a 1966 delivery on a lowheight PDR1/2 chassis, albeit with a normal-height 77-seat body by Neepsend Coachworks of Sheffield. Neepsend was an East Lancs associate, building bus bodies to East Lancs' design between 1963 and 1968. It is seen in 1970. *Ted Jones*

Not all customers built up large fleets of Atlanteans. Caerphilly Urban District Council bought just three – AN68.1Rs with East Lancs 77-seat bodies, received in 1973. This one is seen in 1974, the year when Caerphilly, Bedwas & Machen and Gelligaer UDCs were merged to form Rhymney Valley Council. *Stewart J Brown*

And of course it did, as early Atlantean customers discovered. As we have seen, chassis flexing and cracking under the weight of the 'power pack' at the rear, as well as clutch and gearbox strain, meant that several potentially important customers kept their powder dry until they felt confident about the new model. Bodybuilders too were learning as they went, and after decades of building only for front-engined double-deckers the different stresses of the rear-engined layout were a challenge.

To its credit, Leyland addressed these problems so that by the mid-1960s the Atlantean was a chassis that had been improved on the back of problems experienced by the early customers. With the Bristol VRT and Daimler Fleetline in the Leyland family by the late-1960s, the company had to look hard at what it had on offer. The VRT and Fleetline were not without their problems, single-deck and double-deck Fleetlines being notoriously prone to flexing if the body was insufficiently strong to withstand the stresses. The VRT challenged the rear-engined layout by placing the radiator at the front rather than at the rear as on the Atlantean and Fleetline, and Leyland must have considered a front-mounted radiator when it was pondering the Atlantean's future. It had already supplied export markets with Atlanteans with radiators at the front, but when it launched its greatly improved AN68 series in 1972, the radiator stayed firmly at the rear.

The AN68 saved the Atlantean's reputation and went on to be a hugely successful chassis, notably with the UK's PTE and big city fleets as well as with a growing list of export customers. The fact that bus companies operating in some of the most difficult circumstances – extreme heat, dreadful roads, poor maintenance and chronic overcrowding – chose Atlanteans well into the 1980s is a testament to the soundness of the design. In an era when double-deck bus design was becoming increasingly sophisticated, the relatively straightforward Atlantean still had a very definite role to play.

Chesterfield Corporation bought Atlanteans in 1960 and then in 1971/72, before turning to Daimler Fleetlines and rear-engined single-deckers. This 1971 PDR1A/1 with 73-seat Northern Counties body is seen in 1985. *H J Black*

Although Blackburn-built East Lancs bodies were popular in the north-west of England, there were municipal customers in the south-east, like Eastbourne, which bought East Lancs-bodied Atlanteans until 1980, when it moved on to Dennis Dominators also bodied by East Lancs. This 1972 PDR1A/1, seen in 1973, has a 76-seat East Lancs body. *Stewart J Brown*

What could be the last UK Atlantean still operating for its original owner was this Ipswich Buses 1976 AN68A.1R with 72-seat Roe bodywork converted to open-top layout for City Sightseeing work in the town, seen in 2012. *Tony Wilson*

Many Atlanteans had long lives with their original owners. This 1961 PDR1/1 with semi-lowheight Metro-Cammell body was still in regular use with Ribble as a driver trainer in Blackpool in 1988. *Gavin Booth*

Rhondda Transport was a small BET Group company that was merged into its larger sister, Western Welsh, in 1970. Nine Atlantean PDR1A/1s with Alexander 73-seat bodies had been ordered by Rhondda and were delivered to Western Welsh, but later the Rhondda fleetname was resurrected, as worn in this 1977 view at Cardiff bus station. *Sholto Thomas*

The vehicle choice for the routes of the Ayrshire co-operative AA Motor Services was left to the individual members. Young of Ayr favoured Leylands, and this is a 1976 AN68A.1R Atlantean with 77-seat Northern Counties body at AA's Ayr bus station in 1980. It is in the company of an important former Leyland demonstrator, NTF 9, a 1951 Titan PD2/15 with Leyland bodywork used to demonstrate the new Pneumocyclic gearbox that became available on Leyland double-deck models from 1954. NTF 9 was sold to one of the members of the A1 Service co-operative in 1956 and is now preserved. *Gavin Booth*

Leyland had wanted to replace the Atlantean with its integral Titan TN15, but the sophisticated specification and production problems lost it many potential customers. David Burnicle, who became Engineering Director with Leyland Bus, recalled the priorities of the Passenger Vehicle Department of Leyland Vehicles, as it then was, included launching the Titan into production for LT and the PTEs, and designing a 'rationalised double-deck chassis to replace the Atlantean, Fleetline and VRT, which would complement and supplant the Titan in some of its intended markets by offering a more flexible specification'.

Bristol was given the task of designing and building (initially at least) the Atlantean's true successor, the Olympian. It was unveiled in 1980, just as production of the VRT was being run out, and it went on to be a hugely successful model, first as a Leyland and from 1993 as a Volvo, following the latter's 1988 acquisition of Leyland Bus. It remained in production until 1997.

By 1980, however, former Atlantean customers had other choices in addition to Leyland's new Olympian. They could still buy the Dennis Dominator, the MCW Metrobus, the new Scania N series, or the Volvo Ailsa. While some Atlantean customers looked elsewhere, most recognised the Olympian as its natural successor.

The Atlantean was a popular choice with independent operators, and it often suited bodybuilders to supply bodies tagged on to orders from larger operators. Roe supplied many Atlanteans and Daimler Fleetlines with largely standard body styles, as on this 1975 AN68.1R with 76-seat body to West Yorkshire PTE outline for Cunningham's Bus Service of Paisley, seen in its home town in 1979. *Stewart J Brown*

Two independents based in eastern England – Delaine of Bourne and Whippet of Fenstanton – both bought similar Atlanteans in 1966 and 1973, ordered at the same time and carrying sequential body numbers. This 1966 Willowbrook-bodied PDR1/2 for Delaine was the sister of Whippet's FEW 1D. *Ted Jones*

In 1973, Whippet received this AN68.2R with 83-seat Northern Counties body, seen in Cambridge when new, while Delaine took delivery of similar ACT 540L. *Geoffrey Morant*

The Gotham-based independent South Notts Bus Company, with a requirement for lowheight buses, bought PDR1/3 Atlanteans between 1968 and 1971, but in the absence of a lowheight AN68 variant turned to Daimler Fleetlines – with Leyland engines. This is a 1969 PDR1/3 with 74-seat Northern Counties body, seen in 1979. *Ted Jones*

The important north-east England independent OK Motor Services bought many second-hand double-deckers as well as a handful of new buses for its trunk routes. This is one of three Atlantean AN68.2Rs bought new in 1973 with Northern Counties 83-seat bodies and seen 10 years later. *Gavin Booth*

The PDR1A/1 Special Atlantean was essentially a bridge between the PDR range and the improved AN68 range that would follow later in 1972. This is a 1972 Maidstone & District PDR1A/1 Special, with 78 coach seats in its MCW body, at the Brighton Coach Rally in 1982, liveried for M&D's Invictaway commuter services between Kent and London. *Gavin Booth*

In the early 1990s, several operators had older Atlantean chassis rebodied as single-deckers. This 1978 AN68A.1R, rebodied for Andrews Sheffield Omnibus in 1993 with an East Lancs Sprint 47-seat body, is seen in 1997 at Meadowhall. The chassis was new to East Staffordshire with a 75-seat East Lancs double-deck body. *Tony Wilson*

There would still be some Atlantean activity into the 1990s, though. With operators facing competition following deregulation, there was a move to create low-cost buses that would provide capacity without going to the expense of buying new vehicles. In the early 1980s, Strathclyde PTE had converted eight of its massive Atlantean/Alexander fleet to single-deckers using double-deckers that dated from 1974-77, and these emerged as 31-seaters and 35-seaters. Some were used by the PTE as loan vehicles to smaller operators.

Southampton City Transport had five of its 1974 Atlanteans rebodied by East Lancs as 35-seaters in 1991. The bodies were known as 'Sprint', which hardly matched their performance. Other operators turned to East Lancs in the 1990s for similar bodies on Atlantean chassis – two 46-seaters for Hylton Castle's Catch-A-Bus fleet in 1992, two 47-seaters for the Andrews Sheffield Omnibus fleet in 1992/93, and a 45-seater for Nottingham City Transport in 1994. The Catch-A-Bus vehicles were AN68.2Rs, and the rest AN68.1Rs or AN68A.1Rs. In 1993, Fylde had four former Bradford PDR2/1 Atlanteans, acquired via Hull, rebodied by Northern Counties as 42-seaters.

Strathclyde PTE followed its massive Atlantean fleet with Leyland Olympians, MCW Metrobuses and Volvo Ailsas in the early 1980s. Here, in 1983, a new Olympian with 78-seat lowheight ECW body is pursued in Glasgow by several Alexander-bodied Atlanteans. *Gavin Booth*

When Leyland eventually withdrew the Atlantean from its home market lists, its regular customers had to find another double-deck model. Some stuck with the Atlantean right to the end, but others had already sampled other types in the knowledge that it was on its way out. Leyland's hope was that the 1980-introduced Olympian would be the obvious choice, and certainly the PTEs at Greater Manchester, Merseyside, Strathclyde, Tyne & Wear and West Yorkshire all bought Olympians, but Leyland did not have it all its own way. Merseyside tried small batches of other current models – the Ailsa, Dennis Dominator and Metrobus – before settling on the Olympian and buying large numbers of Leyland Titan TN15s that were surplus to London's requirements. Strathclyde also tried MCW's Metrobus and bought substantial numbers of Volvo's front-engined Ailsa. Tyne & Wear bought only a handful of new double-deckers (MCWs and Scanias) after its last Atlanteans before it was sold in 1986, while West Yorkshire bought Metrobuses alongside Olympians.

South Yorkshire PTE had inherited Sheffield's large Atlantean fleet and bought many of its own examples before it turned to the Dennis Dominator, building up a large fleet. West Midlands PTE had never bought Atlanteans – though its predecessor, Birmingham City Transport, had bought an early batch of 10 before turning to the Daimler Fleetline. After the Fleetline the PTE built up a large fleet of Metrobuses.

Among the larger municipal customers, Grampian, Lothian and Plymouth moved straight on to the Olympian, while Nottingham multi-sourced its double-deckers, buying Dennis Falcon Vs, Leyland Lions, Scanias and Volvo Citybuses as well as Olympians. For NBC companies, the Olympian became the standard double-deck model for most fleets.

Substantial orders were placed for Leyland's Olympian by West Yorkshire PTE to succeed its large fleet of Atlanteans and Fleetlines. Seen here in Leeds, a 1979 Atlantean/Roe is followed by a 1984 Olympian with Roe bodywork. Yorkshire Rider was the arms-length company formed in 1985 by the PTE. *Gavin Booth*

Several of Leyland's export customers went back to single-deckers in a big way, often buying articulated buses to achieve passenger capacity, but CIÉ's successor in Ireland, after a brave but unhappy flirtation with Irish-built buses, turned back to Leyland for the Olympian for its Dublin Bus fleet. Singapore stuck with Leyland, buying a large fleet of Olympians, and more recently Porto has gone back to double-deckers with Berlin-style MANs.

Rear-engined double-deckers would surely have happened in the UK by the 1960s even if Leyland had not paved the way with the Atlantean, but the company's pioneering moves in the 1950s came at the right time for operators looking for increased passenger capacity and the cost savings that could be achieved through driver-only operation. The Atlantean and its successors delivered these things and will long be remembered as one of the most important models in the history of the double-decker.

Open-top Atlanteans were still running for Sevirama in Seville, Spain, in October 2012, including this 38-year-old former Nottingham AN68.1R with open-top East Lancs 76-seat body. The grille behind the front axle is for the air-conditioning unit, an interesting refinement to retro-fit on an open-top bus. *Gavin Booth*

Atlantean bodybuilders

Leyland's original concept for the Atlantean was to sell it as a complete vehicle with Metro-Cammell bodywork. It had worked closely with Metro-Cammell on its Olympic integrally built single-deck range and was enthusiastic about the advantages of integral construction – including weight-saving and structural rigidity – but operators remained sceptical. They still wanted to use their favoured bodybuilders, and larger operators liked to create instantly recognisable body styles.

The Metro-Cammell body on the lowheight integral Atlantean prototypes was attractive and well proportioned, but when the Atlantean was relaunched as a separate chassis, the body styles, although similar, were not as attractive. Metro-Cammell and Alexander were entrusted with the first Atlantean bodies; in normal-height form they were broadly similar, with deeper lower-deck windows in the style of Metro-Cammell's Orion body for front-engined chassis, although the Alexander version had a softer look.

The Roe bodies on early Atlantean chassis were disappointingly ungainly, with more than a hint of MCW styling about them. This is a 77-seat 1962 PDR1/1 for Northern General's Sunderland District fleet, seen in Sunderland in 1970. *Roy Marshall*

MH Coachworks built its first bodies on Atlantean chassis for Belfast Corporation in 1964, like this 77-seat PDR1/2 delivered that year. *Howard Cunningham*

Portsmouth Corporation bought 12 Atlantean PDR2/1s in 1971 and specified Seddon 40-seat single-deck bodies for them. This one is seen in 1979. *Stewart J Brown*

Weymann built the majority of the lowheight bodies for the 344 Atlantean PDR1/1s, with their unusual semi-lowbridge layout on the upper deck, from 1958 through to 1964 when the 'proper' lowheight PDR1/2 model came on the scene. Weymann also built bodies to standard Metro-Cammell designs to relieve capacity at Elmdon, Birmingham, and tended to handle orders for specific customers like Bournemouth, Leeds, Newcastle and Sheffield corporations, and BET's Gateshead & District, Maidstone & District, Trent and Tyneside companies. Weymann also handled more specialised orders, like the 'Gay Hostess' double-deck coach bodies for Ribble and its associates.

Although MCW was heavily involved in bodying early Atlanteans, there were a number of years when no Atlanteans passed through the coachworks. Like Park Royal, MCW preferred to handle larger batches, and after bodying some late PDR1A/1 Atlanteans for London Country and Maidstone & District in 1972/73, its next would be a batch of AN68A.1Rs for Merseyside PTE in 1978, and its last would be AN68A.2Rs for Tyne & Wear PTE, before it concentrated on building complete buses.

Roe was the next builder of the Atlantean, in 1960, with an awkwardly proportioned normal-height body supplied to a number of BET Group companies as well as to municipals like Hull and Sheffield and also to independent operators.

Some of the larger Atlantean customers rebelled against the uninspired looks of the early bodies and worked with bodybuilders to develop their own designs. Liverpool Corporation's large Atlantean fleet carried angular Metro-Cammell bodies with peaks rather than domes, while Glasgow Corporation turned to Alexander for a body using curved glass to good effect. A lowheight version of this style later appeared on PDR1/2 models.

Eastern Coach Works built its first bodies on Atlantean chassis in 1968, and in 1975 supplied bodies on Atlantean AN68.1R chassis to Colchester Borough Transport. The bodies were based on a design developed for South Yorkshire PTE on Daimler Fleetline chassis the previous year, with peaked domes. One of these is seen preparing to leave the ECW plant at Lowestoft in 1975. *Tony Wilson*

The Colchester buses were the only Atlanteans to carry this style of ECW body. One is seen in service when new in 1975. *Gavin Booth*

The next company to body the Atlantean was East Lancs in 1963, with attractive bodies for Bolton Corporation which featured then-fashionable peaked domes. A toned-down version of this became the standard East Lancs double-deck product, also built by its associate Neepsend from 1963.

A few more bodybuilders were added to the Atlantean list in 1964: Northern Counties, with a plain but well-proportioned design; Park Royal, with a fairly plain body style; Willowbrook, which built its first Atlantean bodies on the controversial batch of 22 for Coventry, in the heart of Daimler territory; and MH Coachworks bodied its first Atlanteans for Belfast Corporation in the same year.

Although Park Royal was one of the UK's major bodybuilders, its involvement in bodying Atlanteans was sporadic, and it was best suited to handling large batches of similar bodies. As part of British Leyland it was active in the 1970s bodying Atlanteans for NBC companies, and, in the years before the Park Royal plant closed, for Greater Manchester PTE.

The only double-deck body built by Fowler was mounted on a 1972 Atlantean PDR1/3 chassis for Fishwick of Leyland. The result – not the most attractive of buses – is seen in Preston in 1976. *Gavin Booth*

South Yorkshire PTE developed its own front-end variant of the standard Alexander body. Seen at the Falkirk coachworks ready for delivery in 1979 is a 74-seat AN68A.1R alongside a Bournemouth Transport Fleetline FE30ALR with rounded domes. *Gavin Booth*

Gradually, bodybuilders were moving away from the plain and often badly proportioned bodies of the early Atlanteans to designs that took advantage of the new shapes possible with fibreglass and curved glass screens after opening windscreens were no longer required by law. In Ireland, CIÉ went for dramatically styled bodies on its first Atlanteans, built in its Spa Road works on Metal Sections frames, but when it set up a partnership with Van Hool to build the bodies on its AN68 Atlanteans, it opted for a squarer look.

Marshall first built bodies on the Atlantean in 1968 – three single-deck versions for Great Yarmouth Corporation. Other single-deck Atlanteans were bodied in 1971 by Northern Counties (two ordered by Birkenhead Corporation but delivered to Merseyside PTE) and by Seddon (12 bodies for Portsmouth Corporation).

Some of the last MCW bodies on the Atlantean were built for Tyne & Wear PTE in 1979 – 86-seaters on AN68.2R chassis like this one seen in 1980 in the company of a 1977 Scania/MCW Metropolitan. The Atlantean would be transferred to Northern General with the PTE's other MCW-bodied AN68s in 1982. *Gavin Booth*

After ECW bodies became generally available it built on Atlantean chassis from 1968. Most had bodies that were slightly ungainly normal-height versions of the lowheight body designed for the Bristol VRT, but buses for Colchester Corporation featured peaked domes and a different front-end treatment.

One Atlantean for Leyland-based independent Fishwick had bodywork by W & H Fowler, a local bodybuilder that had been bought by Fishwick. Single-deck Fowler bodies were also built for Fishwick, but the Atlantean body was probably the least attractive for a UK customer.

In the AN68 era most of the main bodybuilders continued to build the Atlantean, often producing versions of what had become a basic style used by several of the main builders. Some of the PTEs developed their own variations on this theme, with Northern Counties and Park Royal producing broadly similar bodies for Greater Manchester, and Roe building its version for West Yorkshire. Alexander built adaptations of its standard AL-type product for Greater Glasgow, Merseyside, South Yorkshire and Tyne & Wear.

The situation changed little through the 1970s to the end of Atlantean home market production in 1984, although MCW and Park Royal built their last Atlantean bodies for the home market in 1979 – MCW because it was moving on to its own Metrobus model, and Park Royal because it was winding down in preparation for closure in 1980. As a result, Northern Counties production increased dramatically, much of it for Greater Manchester, and East Lancs found itself supplying many of the remaining municipal companies in England. In the Atlantean's later years, Alexander, East Lancs, ECW, Northern Counties and Roe were bodying most Atlanteans for the home market, with smaller quantities from builders like Marshall and Willowbrook.

After an unsteady start, the UK bodybuilders got to grips with the shape and proportions of the Atlantean and its Fleetline rival and produced increasingly attractive bodies that had greater passenger appeal – but not without some prodding from the bus companies.

Above: Nottingham City Transport had its own very individual views on double-deck body design for its rear-engined fleet and developed a distinctive and immediately recognisable style that was supplied by various bodybuilders. This is a 1981 Atlantean AN68C.1R with Northern Counties 78-seat dual-door body, seen in 1997. *Tony Wilson*

The Mancunian design by Manchester City Transport represented a fresh look at double-deck bus styling and was produced for Manchester and SELNEC by various bodybuilders. This is one of the first batch, built in 1968 for Manchester by Park Royal on Atlantean PDR1/1 chassis and seen when new. *Ted Jones*

Opposite: This Northern Counties-bodied Atlantean for Nottingham was built to a very different style. The AN68A.1R 79-seater was an exhibit at the 1978 Commercial Show and features a dramatic front-end treatment with Nottingham's trademark narrow entrance and HELP bumper. *Tony Wilson*

Above: Massey built traditionally styled bodies on the Atlantean for the Colchester and Maidstone municipal fleets and the Scottish co-operative, A1 Service. This 1968 Maidstone PDR1/1 with 74-seat body is seen in 1972. *Dale Tringham*

The only Marshall-bodied Atlantean double-deckers were built for South Yorkshire PTE in 1980 on AN68B.1R chassis. This one is at Sheffield. *Tony Wilson*

Testing the Atlantean

When it first appeared, the Leyland Atlantean was so different to everything else on the road that operators wanted to get some experience of it before they committed their hard-earned cash. The trade magazines tested Atlanteans over the years and this was one source of information, but at that time buses were tested in conditions that were slightly artificial as they simulated the loads that buses carried but did not replicate the experience of a bus driven by a range of drivers picking up and dropping passengers in a mix of urban and inter-urban conditions.

Leyland's Atlantean demonstrator KTD 551C with Sheffield-style Park Royal bodywork played a part in convincing fleets like Edinburgh Corporation to choose this model, although Western SMT, which was using it when it was photographed in Glasgow in 1965, never bought new Atlanteans – nor did any other Scottish Bus Group fleet. *Gavin Booth*

After its demonstration duties were over, KTD 551C joined the fleet of Joseph Wood & Son of Mirfield, and is seen operating in Dewsbury in 1977. *H J Black*

The 33ft Atlantean demonstrator MTF 665G, again with Sheffield-style Park Royal body, is seen in 1969 in Huddersfield operating on route 64, which was shared by Bradford and Huddersfield corporations and Hebble. Of these, only Bradford ordered Atlanteans, PDR2/1s like the demonstrator, but with Alexander bodies. *H J Black*

That said, the road-tests in the trade magazine *Bus & Coach* give a flavour of contemporary views. John Dickson-Simpson tested the 1958 James of Ammanford show vehicle and was impressed by the smooth transmission, effective insulation of engine noise and the smooth ride. Its fuel consumption on a four-stops-per-mile basis was 7.2mpg (39.2 litres/100km), and on the open road 11.45mpg (24.7 litres/100km).

Later, noted transport journalist Alan Townsin gave readers a good steer about the Atlantean and its performance. In 1966, he tested Park Royal-bodied PDR1/1 demonstrator KTD 551C, fitted with the 11.1-litre 153bhp 680 engine rather than the 125/130bhp O.600 that was routinely fitted to Atlanteans at the time. On the open road KTD returned an impressive 14.1mpg (20 litres/100km), and 7.85mpg (36 litres/100km) on four-stops-per-mile operation. Townsin found that it was quiet running and pleasant to drive, 'except on twisty roads when the steering became very heavy'.

Townsin tested a later Atlantean for *Bus & Coach* in 1968, Park Royal-bodied PDR2/1 demonstrator MTF 665G, an early example of the longer (and heavier) 33ft (10m) Atlantean. This also had the 680 engine, and a fully automatic gearbox. Fuel consumption was 9.3mpg (30.4 litres/100km) on the open road, and 6.33mpg (44.6 litres/100km) in urban stopping mode. At 30mph cruising speed it returned 12.95mpg (21.8 litres/100km), while the equivalent consumption for KTD 551C was 17.2mpg (16.4 litres/100km). At least the power-assisted steering overcame the problem on twisty roads, but while Townsin found the fully automatic gearbox smooth, he felt it lacked flexibility.

Like the other major manufacturers, Leyland maintained a small fleet of demonstrators that it hawked round potential buyers. There were eight Atlantean demonstrators, plus two LFDDs – one of which, XTC 684, was more of a development vehicle and was never used in service as a demonstrator. As the Atlantean developed, so older demonstrators were sold and new-specification buses took their place.

At the beginning of the Atlantean story, as mentioned earlier, there was LFDD STF 90, which was tested by many British fleets, as was integral Atlantean 281 ATC, and then there came a raft of demonstrators as the Atlantean chassis went into production. There was normal-height 398 JTB and semi-lowbridge 661 KTJ; 460 MTE was built for Birmingham City Transport and attracted a single order for 10 more; and 46 LTB, which was re-registered 8985 XI in Northern Ireland for use by Ulster Transport Authority, and later that year became HZA 723 when it transferred to CIÉ in Dublin.

A later demonstrator was SGD 669, a standard Glasgow Corporation Atlantean, which was bought from Glasgow when almost new in 1963 to join the Leyland fleet. Two more demonstrators were 1965 Park Royal-bodied PDR1/1 KTD 551C and Park Royal-bodied PDR2/1 MTF 665G, mentioned above.

The weekly trade paper *Commercial Motor* conducted a long-term in-service test of a London Country Atlantean AN68A.1R with Roe body. Two similar buses are seen at Amersham Garage in 1981. *Tony Wilson*

Although Leyland built no AN68-series demonstrators, arrangements were made on occasion to loan one operator's vehicle to another to allow them to gain first-hand experience. The weekly trade publication *Commercial Motor* conducted a long-term test involving a London Country Atlantean AN68A.1R from its delivery in 1980 and found that it ran with monotonous reliability, returning a fuel consumption of 8.9mpg (31.7 litres/100km). Writing in *Commercial Motor*, Noel Millier said, 'The reliability of the Atlantean over the last two years has been such that the Leyland Olympians which are to replace them will have a lot to live up to.'

While most operators would test an Atlantean in service on a busy route – sometimes one that did not stray too far from a company depot – others organised comparison tests to establish the type of double-decker best suited to local conditions. Halifax Corporation conducted comparison tests in 1965, pitching two Atlanteans, demonstrator SGD 669 and a 1961 Wallasey bus, against a Daimler Fleetline and eight front-engined double-deckers – an AEC Renown, Albion Lowlander, Dennis Loline, Guy Arab V and Routemaster, plus three buses from the Halifax fleet – an AEC Regent V, Daimler CVG6 and Leyland Titan PD3.

Halifax's General Manager, Geoffrey Hilditch, wrote that 'generally speaking, our staff and passengers were pleased with [SGD 669's] performance', but noted that there was a feeling that it was 'a little underpowered for our requirements'. Its fuel consumption, 9.45mpg (29.9 litres/100km), was better than the Fleetline's 9.27mpg (30.5 litres/100km), but both were bettered by the Halifax CVG6 at 9.8mpg (28.8 litres/100km), though Atlantean SGD 669 was second. The Wallasey Atlantean was poorest at 8.36mpg (33.8 litres/100km). However, in spite of this, Halifax never ordered Atlanteans and turned to Fleetlines.

Edinburgh Corporation also conducted comparison tests in 1965, pitching new Atlantean demonstrator KTD 551C against a Fleetline and a Renown, with an Edinburgh Titan PD3 for comparison. Here the Renown returned the best fuel consumption, 8.56mpg (33 litres/100km), followed by the PD3 with 8.46mpg (33.4 litres/100km), and with the Atlantean at 8.2mpg (34.4 litres/100km) and Fleetline at 8.25mpg (34.2 litres/100km) very close behind. Edinburgh wanted to split its next order between Atlanteans and Fleetlines, but played safe with Atlanteans and PD3s before standardising on the Atlantean for the next 15 years.

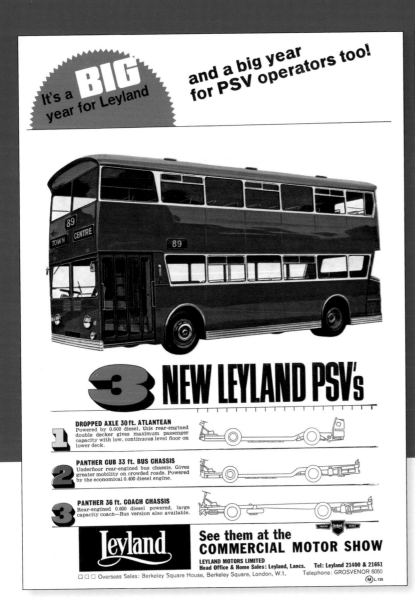

The Atlantean in adverts

In the 1950s and 1960s, when bus chassis and body manufacturers had so much to play for, the trade weekly and monthly magazines always included many pages of advertising. Leyland, as one of the UK's principal bus builders, advertised widely, and it is interesting to follow the progress of the Atlantean through some of these adverts.

Above left: For the 1964 Commercial Show, Leyland advertising was featuring its three new models – the drop-axle PDR1/2 Atlantean, and the new rear-engined single-deck Panther and Panther Cub, illustrated by a Liverpool Corporation MCW-bodied PDR1/1.

Above right: In this 1965 advert, Leyland showed a real PDR1/2, a newly delivered example with Alexander 74-seat body for East Midland, which received the first examples of this Atlantean variant.

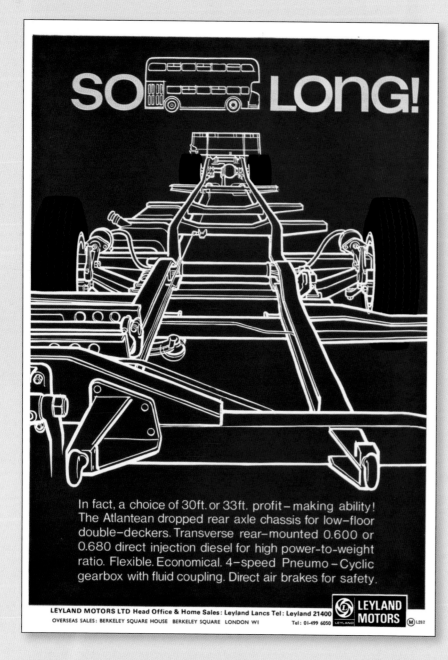

SO LONG!

In fact, a choice of 30ft. or 33ft. profit – making ability! The Atlantean dropped rear axle chassis for low–floor double–deckers. Transverse rear–mounted 0.600 or 0.680 direct injection diesel for high power–to–weight ratio. Flexible. Economical. 4–speed Pneumo – Cyclic gearbox with fluid coupling. Direct air brakes for safety.

LEYLAND MOTORS LTD Head Office & Home Sales: Leyland Lancs Tel: Leyland 21400
OVERSEAS SALES: BERKELEY SQUARE HOUSE BERKELEY SQUARE LONDON WI   Tel: 01-499 6050

LEYLAND MOTORS

Leyland promoted the choice of 30ft and 33ft Atlantean chassis in this 1967 advert.

Intriguingly, Leyland seemed a bit coy about the Atlantean when it first appeared in integral form in 1956. There was one advert late in 1956 following the launch at the Commercial Show, describing the Atlantean as 'The bus with *your* ideas ... but built by *us*,' noting that its reception at the show was 'highly gratifying to us' and concluding, 'All in all, the general consensus of opinion supported the view of the trade press that the Atlantean "initiated a major trend in double-deck layout".' This was undoubtedly true, but the feedback from operators caused Leyland to rush back to the drawing-board to revamp it as a chassis, and suddenly everything went quiet for a couple of years as far as Leyland's advertising was concerned.

The next indication that something was happening came from MCW, which advertised the Atlantean in mid-1958 with a doctored photo showing an Atlantean that was much closer to the models that were to be unveiled at the Commercial Show later in the year, with a 'bustle' for the engine compartment but with the lower front panel of the 1956 prototype.

Leyland was advertising the improved MkII Atlantean in 1962, using a photo of one of Liverpool's large order and describing the improvements to the entrance and seating layout that had been carried out, though with little reference to mechanical improvements.

In 1963, Leyland adverts were proclaiming that there were 'Nearly 150,000,000 miles of experience' behind the MkII Atlantean, listing 'new up-to-date reliability features' including better support brackets for the engine, quick-access hatches for frequently used engine parts, a new fluid flywheel and lock-up clutch, a repositioned gear control, and other improvements that resulted from the feedback from operators of the early chassis.

The drop-centre rear axle Atlantean, the PDR1/2, was announced in adverts at the time of the 1964 Commercial Show, and the 33ft PDR2/1 was featured in adverts coinciding with the same show in 1966.

From that time, Atlantean advertising became more general, but the growth of British Leyland meant that there was very little in the way of competition for its models, so there was less need to advertise. Added to that, the main trade monthly *Bus & Coach* was struggling as a consequence of the lack of advertising income, and the magazine ceased publication in 1970.

With the New Bus Grants scheme in mind, this 1969 advert emphasises the suitability of the fully automatic Atlantean for driver-only operation, illustrated by a Plymouth Corporation PDR2/1 with Park Royal two-door bodywork.

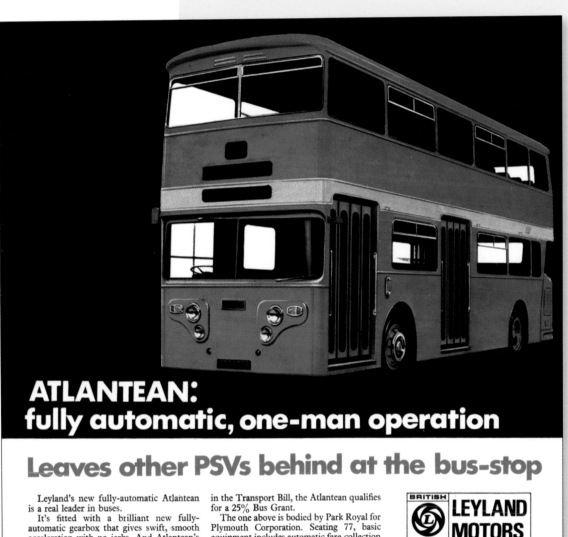

ATLANTEAN:
fully automatic, one-man operation

Leaves other PSVs behind at the bus-stop

Leyland's new fully-automatic Atlantean is a real leader in buses.

It's fitted with a brilliant new fully-automatic gearbox that gives swift, smooth acceleration with no jerks. And Atlantean's specially designed for one-man operation, which helps bring down operating costs. That's apart from Leyland reliability and toughness which help cut down maintenance.

Big bonus, too. Under proposals outlined in the Transport Bill, the Atlantean qualifies for a 25% Bus Grant.

The one above is bodied by Park Royal for Plymouth Corporation. Seating 77, basic equipment includes automatic fare collection machines and Sekonic passenger computers. Reliable power comes from the Leyland 680 Diesel.

So with the great new Atlantean around, **why settle for less?**

LEYLAND MOTORS

Head Office & Home Sales: Leyland, Preston PR5 1SN, England. Tel: Leyland 21400
Overseas Sales: Berkeley Square House, Berkeley Square, London W.1. Telephone: 01-499 6050

Atlantean specifications

1954 Prototype (STF 90)

Length	27ft
Wheelbase	17ft 2¾in
Engine	O.350
Power output	115bhp @ 2,200rpm
Displacement	5.7 litres
Brakes	Air
Gearbox	Wilson preselect
Suspension	Independent front suspension, rear coil/leaf springs

1956 Prototype PDR1 (281 ATC)

Length	9.09m
Wheelbase	4.95m
Engine	O.600
Power output	125bhp @ 1,800rpm
Displacement	9.8 litres
Brakes	Air-hydraulic
Gearbox	4-speed Pneumocyclic (air shift)
Suspension	Independent front suspension, rear leaf springs

1958-1968 PDR1/1

Length	9.14m
Wheelbase	4.95m
Engine	O.600
Power output	125bhp @ 1,800rpm/140bhp @ 1,700rpm
Displacement	9.8 litres
Brakes	Air
Gearbox	4-speed Pneumocyclic (electric shift)
Suspension	Leaf springs front and rear

1966-1971 PDR2/1

Length	9.9m
Wheelbase	5.64m
Engine	680
Power output	153bhp @ 1,750rpm/165bhp @ 1,900rpm
Displacement	11.1 litres
Brakes	Air
Gearbox	4-speed Pneumocyclic (air shift)
Suspension	Leaf springs front and rear

1972-1976 AN68.1R

Length	9.42m
Wheelbase	4.95m
Engine	680
Power output	153bhp @ 1,750rpm
Displacement	11.1 litres
Brakes	Air
Gearbox	4-speed Pneumocyclic (air shift)
Suspension	Leaf springs front and rear

1982-1984 AN68D.2R

Length	10.13m
Wheelbase	5.64m
Engine	680
Power output	174bhp @ 1,900rpm
Displacement	11.1 litres
Brakes	Air
Gearbox	5-speed Pneumocyclic (air shift)
Suspension	Leaf springs front and rear

Above: Atlanteans from the English PTE fleets were snapped up by other operators when they became surplus to requirements, often at the time of bus service deregulation in 1986. This former Tyne & Wear PTE AN68A.2R with 86-seat MCW body was new in 1979, was transferred to National Bus Company's Northern General fleet just three years later, and reached the independent OK Travel via another local independent, Hunter of Seaton Delaval. It is seen in West Auckland in 1995. *Gavin Booth*

Greater Manchester PTE disposed of many Leyland Atlanteans at the time of deregulation in 1986 and most found new homes. This 1972 Atlantean AN68.1R with Park Royal body passed from Greater Manchester Transport to the newly privatised Ribble company in 1987; it is seen in Bolton in 1988. *Gavin Booth*

Index

A Hornsby 53
A1 Service 35
AA Motor Services 35
Aberdeen 40. 53
Accrington 40, 53
AEC 4, 24, 26, 27, 45, 58, 69, 72
AEC Q 6
AEC Regent 26
AEC Regent RT 48
AEC Regent V 72, 104
AEC Renown 104
AEC Routemaster 8, 10, 24, 26, 35, 104
Albion Lowlander 104
Alexander 16, 17, 24, 34, 51, 53, 75, 76, 89, 93, 98
Alexander (Belfast) 53
Alexander AL-type 98
Ammanford 16, 103
Andrews Sheffield Omnibus 89
Arriva 67
Ashton-under-Lyne 35
Atlantis 13
Atlas 13
Australia 26, 68, 72

Baco 75
Baghdad 51, 72
Bamber Bridge Motor Services 31
Barrow 66
Bedford 47
Bedwas & Machen 53
Belfast 24, 53, 96
Berlin 91
BET Group 4, 10, 14, 16, 34, 40, 47, 95
Birkenhead 40, 97
Birmingham 6, 9, 21, 31, 34, 47, 90, 103
Blackburn 40, 67
Blackpool 53, 67
Bolton 31, 34, 96
Bombay 68
Bournemouth 35, 95
Bradford 40, 89
Brighton 48
Bristol 4, 7, 27, 45, 58, 85
Bristol Lodekka 7, 14
Bristol VRT 27, 45, 50, 51, 53, 58, 82, 85, 98
British Leyland 27, 45, 72, 96, 107
British Motor Holdings 27

British Overseas Airways Corporation (BOAC)....35, 40
Buckmaster 11
Burnicle, David 85
Burton on Trent 53
Bury 31
Bus & Coach 10, 13, 103, 107
Busaf 68, 76
Buses Illustrated 4, 10, 13

C S Pegg 53
Caerphilly 53
Caerphilly UDC 53
Calypso, Gibraltar 72
Catch-A-Bus 89
Ceylon 68
Chesterfield 22
City Tramways, Cape Town 68
Colchester 40, 98
Commercial Motor 104
Commercial Motor Show 1954 10
Commercial Motor Show 1956 ....13, 106
Commercial Motor Show 1958 ....17, 24, 106
Commercial Motor Show 1964 106
Commercial Motor Show 1966 ....40, 106
Córas Iompair Éireann (CIÉ) 34, 68, 71, 91, 97, 103
Coventry 34, 57, 96
Cuba 68
Cunningham's Bus Service 40

DAF 71
Daimler 4, 6, 24, 45, 96
Daimler CV range 26
Daimler CVG6 104
Daimler Fleetline 4, 14, 15, 16, 24, 26, 27, 31, 34, 35, 37, 45, 50, 51, 57, 58, 66, 82, 104
Dalfa 69
DAMRI, Surabaya 76
Delaine Coaches 35
Delhi 68
Democratic Republic of the Congo 72
Denmark 68
Dennis 4, 24
Dennis Dominator 57, 85, 90
Dennis Falcon V 90
Dennis Loline 104
Devon General 10, 21, 22, 24

Dickson-Simpson, John 103
Dublin 103
Dublin Bus 91
Dunfermline 51, 76
Duple Metsec 75, 76

Earls Court 10, 13
East Kent 53
East Lancs 34, 89, 96, 98
East Midland 21
East Staffordshire 53
Eastbourne 48
Eastern Coach Works (ECW) 7, 14, 27, 45, 53, 58, 76, 98
Edinburgh 4, 9, 35, 53, 104
Elmdon, Birmingham 16, 95
England, Ben 13

F Proctor & Son 53
Far East 75, 76
Farington 66
FFG 71
First Group 67
First Manchester 67
Friedmann & Maier fuel pump 60
Fylde 53, 89

Gardner 6LXB engine 51
Garelochhead Coach Services 48
Gateshead & District 24, 95
Gay Hostess 24, 95
Gelligaer 53
Germany 72
Glasgow 4, 11, 16, 17, 24, 34, 69, 95, 103
GM Buses 66
Graham's Bus Services 31
Grampian 53, 66, 90
Great Yarmouth 22, 35, 40, 97
Greater Glasgow PTE 56, 57, 66
Greater Manchester 66
Greater Manchester PTE 56, 66, 90, 96, 98
Guy 4, 6, 24, 26, 45
Guy Arab 26
Guy Arab V 104

H W Hunter & Sons 48
Halifax 104

Halls of Hounslow 40
Hamburg 71
Hamilton 22
Haslingden 53
Hayter, G W 13
Heathrow Airport 40
Hilditch, Geoffrey 104
Hong Kong 37, 75
Hull...22, 66, 89, 95
Hylton Castle 89
Hyndburn 53

India 68
Indonesia 68, 76
Ipswich 40
Iran 26, 72
Iranian Revolution 76
Iraq 72
Ireland 21, 68, 71

J Fishwick & Sons 31, 67, 76, 98
J James 16, 21, 24, 103
J Laurie...22
J Rennie 51, 76
Jack, Doug...15
Jaguar 26

Kenya 68
King Alfred Motor Services..................................40
Kinshasa 72
Kuwait Transport Co 76

Leeds...34, 35, 40, 95
Leicester 31
Leighton Buzzard 11
Leyland 6, 9, 11, 14, 15, 21, 26, 27, 29, 34, 45, 47,
57, 58, 60, 66, 68, 69, 71, 76, 80, 82, 85,
90, 91, 93, 98, 103, 104, 105, 106
Leyland 'Low Floor Double Deck Chassis'
(LFDD) 9, 10, 11, 13, 80, 103
Leyland Atlantean...........4, 5, 7, 11, 14, 16, 17, 21, 24,
26, 27, 29, 31, 34, 35, 45, 50, 53, 57, 60, 66,
67, 68, 69, 71, 72, 75, 76, 80, 82, 89,
90, 91, 93, 95, 96, 97, 98, 103,
105, 106, 107
Leyland 690 engine.....................................51,76
Leyland Atlantean AN68.........4, 50, 51, 53, 56. 67, 80,
82, 97, 98, 104
Leyland Atlantean AN68.1R 50, 51, 71, 89, 95
Leyland Atlantean AN68.2L 51, 76
Leyland Atlantean AN68.2R 50, 51, 53, 89
Leyland Atlantean AN68A.....................................60
Leyland Atlantean AN68A.1R..........................89, 104
Leyland Atlantean AN68A.2L..............................74

Leyland Atlantean AN68A.2R.............................76, 95
Leyland Atlantean AN68B..60
Leyland Atlantean AN68C..60
Leyland Atlantean AN68D..60
Leyland Atlantean AN68D.2R.................................76
Leyland Atlantean AN69...76
Leyland Atlantean AN69.2L.....................................76
Leyland Atlantean AN69.2L.....................................76
Leyland Atlantean AN69.2R.....................................76
Leyland Atlantean LPDR1..50
Leyland Atlantean MkII...31
Leyland Atlantean PDR1 ....15, 50
Leyland Atlantean PDR1/1 ....16, 37, 71, 95, 103
Leyland Atlantean PDR1/2 ....34, 40, 95, 106
Leyland Atlantean PDR1/3 ....40, 51
Leyland Atlantean PDR1A/1 ....40, 95
Leyland Atlantean PDR1A/1 Special 50
Leyland Atlantean PDR2/1 ....40, 53, 89, 103, 106
Leyland B45 58
Leyland Bus...85
Leyland Bus, The 15
Leyland Cub 6, 11
Leyland G2 gearbox 60
Leyland Leopard 72
Leyland Lion..26
Leyland Lowloader 9
Leyland MkII Atlantean 106
Leyland National 26, 47, 49, 58
Leyland O.350 engine...13
Leyland O.400 engine...26
Leyland O.600 engine...............6, 7, 9, 13, 26, 31, 103
Leyland O.680/680 engine.......24, 26, 37, 40, 60, 76, 103
Leyland Olympian 58, 71, 76, 85, 90, 104
Leyland Olympic 7
Leyland Panther..26, 69
Leyland Panther Cub 26
Leyland Passenger Transport Board 6
Leyland Royal Tiger 7
Leyland Tiger 7
Leyland Tiger Cub 7
Leyland Titan 4, 7, 13, 24, 26, 58, 68, 71
Leyland Titan PD1 6
Leyland Titan PD2 6
Leyland Titan PD3 ....13, 71, 104
Leyland Titan TN15 ....85, 90
Leyland Worldmaster 26
Leyland-Albion Lowlander 34
Lincoln 35
Lisbon 69
Liverpool 22, 34, 47, 95, 106
London 24, 26, 40, 58, 66
London Country Bus Services....48, 50, 53, 66, 95, 104
London RT-family 6

London Transport (LT) 4, 6, 8, 11, 24, 26, 35, 48,
57, 58, 75, 85, 90
London Transport Country Area 48
Lothian 53, 66, 67, 90
Lowestoft 58
Lowland Motorways 11
Lytham St Annes 48, 53

Maidstone 35
Maidstone & District 16, 21, 22, 24, 50, 95
MAN 91
Manchester 11, 34, 40, 47, 48
Mancunian 48
Marshall 40, 97, 98
Martins & Caetano 69
Massey 35
MCW Metrobus 57, 85, 90, 98
Merseyside PTE 40, 48, 56, 66, 67, 90, 95, 97, 98
Metal Sections...97
Metro Manila...76
Metro-Cammell 11, 17, 21, 22, 24, 34, 47, 68, 95
Metro-Cammell Olympic 93
Metro-Cammell Orion 16, 93
Metropolitan-Cammell-Weymann
(MCW)...............................16, 69, 95, 98, 106
Metsec 75
Metsec/CIÉ 71
Mexborough & Swinton 21
MH Coachworks 96
Midland General..53
Midland Red (BMMO).................................4, 6, 7, 24
Millier, Noel 104
MIRA...15
Müller, Dr-Ing A 9

National Bus Company (NBC)......26, 47, 53, 58, 90, 96
Neepsend 34, 96
Neoplan..72
New Bus Grants 27, 47, 53
New South Wales Department of
Government Transport, Sydney........................72
New York Metropolitan Transportation Authority....74
New Zealand..26
Newcastle 4, 22, 24, 47, 95
Newport 35
North West Museum of Transport 11
North-east England 4
North-west England...24
Northern Counties 34, 40, 76, 89, 96, 97, 98
Northern General.....................................4, 13, 21, 22, 24, 53, 66
Northern Ireland..103
Nottingham City Transport 13, 35, 66, 89, 90

Oldham 35
OTCZ 72

Pakistan 68
Park Royal 34, 37, 45, 53, 58, 69, 72, 74, 95, 96, 98, 103
Passenger Transport Executives (PTEs) 47, 48, 56, 57, 82, 85, 98
Persian Gulf 76
Philippines 76
Plymouth 22, 40, 90
Pneumocyclic gearbox 7, 11, 13, 40
Porto 69, 91
Porton Down 22
Portsmouth 31, 40, 66, 97
Portugal 69
Potteries 10, 22
PPD, Jakarta 76
Preston 22, 53, 67
Pretoria 68, 76
PTS, Baghdad 72

Quito, Ecuador 76

Rawtenstall 53
Rhondda 40
Rhymney Valley 53
Ribble 10, 22, 24, 53, 66, 67, 95
Road Transport Industry Training Board 40
Roe 45, 53, 98
Rossendale 53

Salford 31
Salvador Caetano 69
San Francisco 74
Saudi Arabia 72
Scania 47, 90
Scania/MCW Metropolitan 57
Scottish Bus Group 4, 34
Scottish Omnibuses 11
Scout Motor Services 22
Seddon 40, 47
Self-Changing Gears Ltd, Coventry 7, 21
SELNEC PTE 48, 56
Sheffield 22, 24, 40, 90, 95
Silver Star Motor Services 22
Singapore 91
Singapore Bus Service 75
Smith, E J 10, 13
South Africa 68, 76
South Notts Bus Company 40
South Wales Transport 24
South Yorkshire Motors 31
South Yorkshire PTE 56, 57, 69, 98

Southall 58
Southampton 40, 66, 67
Southampton City Transport 89
Southdown 10, 53
Southport 53
Spa Road 71, 97
Spain 26, 68
St Helens 11
Stagecoach 67
Standerwick 24
Stockholm 69
Stockton 35
Stratford Blue 40
Strathclyde PTE 56, 66, 89, 90
Strowger 11
Sunbeam 12
Sunderland District 24
SVAR, Tehran 76

Tagus, River 69
Teesside 40
Tehran 51, 72
Tehran Omnibus Board 72
Thomas McArdle Ltd 71
Tilling Group 47
Townsin, Alan 103
Trans World Airlines 40
Transport Act 1968 27
Trent 22, 24, 53, 95
Turkey 26
Tyne & Wear PTE 56, 57, 90, 95, 98
Tyneside 95
Tyneside PTE 48

Uganda 68
Ulster Transport Authority 103
Ulsterbus 53
United States of America 5, 26
UTIC 69

Van Hool 71, 97
Van Hool McArdle 71
Voith 69
Volvo 7, 85
Volvo Ailsa 57, 85, 90
Volvo Citybus 90

W & H Fowler 98
W Gash & Sons 53
Wallasey 16, 22, 24, 104
Walsall 12, 22
Warrington 53
Weardale Motor Services 48

West Midlands 24
West Midlands PTE 56, 57
West Riding Automobile 35
West Yorkshire PTE 56, 90, 98
Western Welsh 22
Weymann, Addlestone 16, 21, 22, 24, 95
Whippet Coaches 35, 72
White Ladies 24
Wigan 40
Willowbrook 34, 72, 96, 98
Wilson pre-selector gearbox 9
Workington 47
Workington 58
World War 2 6

Yorkshire Woollen District 40, 53

Zaire 72